T0352671

Rosemary Waugh

Rosemary Waugh is an award-winning art critic and journalist, specialising in theatre, dance and visual art. Her reviews, interviews and essays have been published by titles including *The New Statesman*, *Condé Nast Traveller*, the *Financial Times*, *The i*, the *Evening Standard*, the *Independent*, *Time Out*, *The Stage*, *Exeunt*, *Artists and Illustrators*, *OOF*, *The English Garden*, the *Dance Gazette*, the *Globe* and *Art UK*. She is also the author of an extensive collection of theatre programme notes for shows on in the West End. rosemarywaugh.com

Rosemary Waugh

Running the Room

Conversations with Women Theatre Directors

NICK HERN BOOKS
London
www.nickhernbooks.co.uk

A Nick Hern Book

Running the Room
first published in Great Britain in 2023
by Nick Hern Books Limited,
The Glasshouse, 49a Goldhawk Road, London W12 8QP

Copyright © 2023 Rosemary Waugh

Rosemary Waugh has asserted her right
to be identified as the author of this work

Cover image: Kiln Theatre, London (front cover); Manchester
Royal Exchange, Lyric Hammersmith and Leeds Playhouse (back
cover; top to bottom); all photos by Helen Murray/ArenaPAL for
the Our Empty Theatres project, May–July 2020
(www.arenapal.com)

Designed and typeset by Nick Hern Books, London
Printed and bound in the UK by Great Britain by 4Edge, Essex

A CIP catalogue record for this book
is available from the British Library

ISBN 978 1 83904 040 5

For Lucian and Leo, always

Contents

CONTENTS

CONTENTS

Introduction

This is a book of many voices. It is not a set of rules or a checklist of 'things to do' when directing a play. Nor is it a manifesto promoting one approach to making theatre above another. Indeed, if it has a theme, it is this: there is no right way to be a theatre director. Or rather, there are as many ways of being a (female) theatre director as there are (female) theatre directors. What I often enjoyed most about talking to the brilliant creatives represented here was discovering how passionate they are about doing the exact opposite to one another. Or, in a less extreme way, doing a million different variations of each other's practice.

At one point in the extended interviewing process, I became preoccupied by asking different people the same questions on, for example, the role of the text or their opinions on using personal material in the rehearsal room, just to hear the contrary views that would filter back to me. The resulting edited interviews are, in fact, far more varied in their questions than that, with each interview focusing on a particular facet of each director's practice. This includes discussing running a theatre in an era of upheaval with Vicky Featherstone, the creation of a visual vocabulary with Ola Ince, the beauty of movement with Rebecca Frecknall, and the use of culturally specific details with Indhu Rubasingham.

The book opens with a dialogue between past and present, with Carrie Cracknell discussing her continued forays into working with adaptations of classic texts. It then moves on to the therapeutic values of theatre, with Nadia Fall, before opening outwards to cover everything from politics to playfulness to playing games in rehearsal. It ends with Sarah Frankcom's call to find confidence in being uniquely yourself. Sometimes, as with three early chapters all relating to physicality (Rebecca Frecknall, Yaël Farber and Nancy Medina), I have deliberately grouped together complementary reflections. At others, like with Debbie Hannan and Jenny Sealey's respective comments on disability and theatre, I've deliberately separated out topics to emphasise the variability in ideas and approaches relating to similar issues.

The one constant is that, across all the chapters, you will see the multitudinous ways of creating work for the stage. Take, for example, the idea of 'the text' and the reverence given to the exact words printed in a script. For some, like Lynette Linton, the play itself is king and what's known as 'table work' is a must (or, as she put it, 'magical'). But for others, like, most memorably, Emma Rice, tables are made for dancing on, and getting everyone sitting down with paperwork-in-hand is anathema to making good art. And, even amongst the text-worshippers, there's much debate to be had about what lines you cut or edit, when and how.

I began the book in 2021, in the other-worldly era of the coronavirus pandemic. The enforced break gave me an unplanned but useful opportunity to take stock of my career and commit to a project long bubbling away at the back of my mind. As a journalist and critic, I frequently have the pleasure of interviewing artists and performers about the amazing, inspiring, and sometimes infuriating work they make. These discussions are almost always fascinating, no matter what my personal artistic tastes and preferences are. Talking about theatre is the best job because the conversation can go to so many different places. There is a never-ending supply of things to say about both the contents of a play itself – the location, the historical backdrop, the themes and all the things a director is planning to do with it – and how a person approaches making theatre in general, both practically and philosophically.

However, the conventions of journalism and the task of producing a normally short-ish article that is almost always tied to the opening of a new show, means that so much of those conversations remained buried in an archive of transcripts on my laptop. It was all this other 'stuff' – the 'stuff' that was often classed as too niche (or too 'theatre geek', as I prefer) for a wide audience – that I normally found the most interesting. It was here that a director would start sharing intricate details of their founding inspirations, approaches and techniques. To reference Yaël Farber's interview here, these were not the kind of details relevant to 'the capitalist contemporary pursuit of selling theatre'. These were studious, thoughtful and affecting reflections on an artist's own practice, developed over years of creating work.

Prior to starting the project, I sought out existing books on the topic. I discovered that the few collections that did exist were either out of date, or focused on a different cohort (for example, international or US-based) than the people I wanted to interview. I wish I had a more interesting answer to why I wanted to make a book about the UK's leading contemporary female directors than: there wasn't one. But that was a big part of it. I found it outrageous that the expertise of so many exceptional artistic minds would not be present if, for example, you were a student on the lookout for a book about directing. This included the women who had run many of the nation's most important theatres and companies for decades, and the women who created a significant portion of the work performed on those stages.

The argument for writing a book that focuses solely on women is, of course, more complex than that. Although I think a glaring blank in the existing literature tells a convincing story of its own. Several years ago, I made a conscious decision in my own interviewing practice to avoid asking interviewees questions based on demographic characteristics. Put more crudely, I wanted to avoid ever again asking a young, Black, female director questions about being a young, Black, female director. While being absolutely open to discussing age, race and gender, I wanted to break away from a reductionist practice which unfairly burdens artists who are not older, white and male with having their work viewed solely through the prism of identity. To borrow Katie Mitchell's observation, Sam Mendes is not asked what it is like to be a male director (although maybe he should be).

So, to write a book about specifically female directors perhaps runs counter to this ideal. One rule I came up with – and then promptly broke, particularly when talking to Katie Mitchell and Marianne Elliott – was not to ask any questions about feminism, femaleness or femininity. I wanted to approach everyone's artistic practice in the same way that a male director's practice would be approached. But the problem is: gender is relevant. And, in my opinion, fascinating. Many of the women represented here, as with other directors I have interviewed elsewhere, explore the concept in their own work and use feminist principles to underpin how and why they make art. Many have also experienced how their gender has impacted on their working life, from one-to-one interactions backstage to job offers given or withheld.

The question of whether being female is a barrier to success in the theatre industry is an interesting one. When I approached the Society of London Theatre (SOLT) for recent statistics on female directors, I was told that 58% of the plays submitted for the 2023 Olivier Awards (eligibility period 21 February 2022 – 14 February 2023) were directed by female-identifying directors. That sounds pretty great, although the numbers fell sharply for musicals (only 18% by female-identifying directors) and 'entertainment or comedy plays' (25% by female-identifying directors). SOLT's remit covers London's top and mid-sized theatres, including West End venues and places like the National Theatre, Old Vic and Young Vic, Donmar Warehouse and Royal Court Theatre. To be eligible for an Olivier Award, a show simply needs to be on at a SOLT venue for more than the minimum number of performances each category states. In the case of plays, they must have a run of more than thirty performances to be in with a chance of winning an award.

That 58% suggests women directors are well represented in the industry and in line to receive its biggest accolades. Yet if we look at one of the awards those women could win, the Sir Peter Hall Award for Best Director at the Olivier Awards, the other side of the picture presents itself. Since its inauguration in 1976, this award has only been won by five women: Deborah Warner (1988), Marianne Elliott (2013 and 2020), Lyndsey Turner (2014), Miranda Cromwell (2020, alongside Elliott) and Rebecca Frecknall (2022). Despite being a significant and integral part of the British theatre industry, the work of female directors remains overlooked and undervalued when compared to their male counterparts – although the dates of those female winners suggest this is improving. This tallies with what I've been repeatedly told when interviewing female directors over the years: gender is both irrelevant and relevant. Which, if nothing else, certainly makes it worthy of continued conversation.

Deciding who to include in this book was a 'problem' I was largely happy to have. The wealth of talented female directors working in British theatre meant the book could have easily contained twice the number of interviewees, or more. The aim was to capture the diversity of the women working in the theatre industry in terms of age, race, geographical and economic background, non-disabled and living with a disability, and the type of theatre they make. I also wanted to include a combination of artistic directors and freelance practitioners, and a mixture of people predominantly working in London and throughout the wider UK, and those who also work internationally. Necessarily, there are omissions and gaps, hopefully not too many egregious ones. Flat-out schedules – directors tend to be exceptionally busy people – meant that not all the women approached were able to spare the time, but I was overwhelmed by the generosity and enthusiasm received from all those who feature here.

This collection also includes two trans women directors, Jamie Fletcher and Emma Frankland, and one non-binary director, Debbie Hannan, who uses the pronouns she/her and they/them. Hannan was happy to be included in a book with this title because they felt that being assigned female at birth had a significant impact on their career, both in positive and negative ways. As Jamie Fletcher notes in her interview, there are few trans female directors currently working in mid- and large-scale theatres. The rise in the number of female directors working at the highest level in recent decades has been noticeable – and indeed is part of the argument for this book. I wonder, were we to create another volume of this book in ten or fifteen years' time, if the number of trans and gender non-conforming directors will have also risen. If it has, or hasn't, it would be interesting to then look at what these directors are being commissioned to direct and at which venues. For example, are they only being approached by theatres to direct work with an obvious link to gender or trans identities and, if so, how do they feel about that?

I conducted the first of the interviews, with Natalie Abrahami, in 2021 when the pandemic was still very much raging, and the last one, with Marianne Elliott, in spring 2023, when it felt like an odd fever dream. It's fair to say that the pandemic and its devastating impact on the industry hung like a cloud over many of the conversations I had during these years, especially for the artistic directors trying to keep their theatres afloat. So as not to date the text too much, I have tried to keep direct mentions of the pandemic to a minimum, but, of course, there are aspects of the conversations tied to when they took place, either because of the global events underpinning them or because they relate to a specific moment in an artist's career. It's quite possible, and usual, for a person's thinking on a topic to evolve and change over time.

But to return to that overarching theme. The edited conversations reproduced here contain a great array of advice and information that will remain useful and interesting for years to come. Most of it is focused on the 'how': how these directors talk to actors, how they create a certain environment in a rehearsal space, how they work with a living playwright, how they run the room. Intermingled with this is the 'why': why they approach a text in this way, why they never ask for personal information, why they ever entered a theatre in the first place... It's not a 'do-this' doctrine, but a multicoloured patchwork of insights gleaned from Britain's most ferocious, fearless and creative female directors. These are the words of women who, to paraphrase Sarah Frankcom, weren't ever content to just sit there, silently.

Carrie Cracknell

Great plays and great actors

Carrie Cracknell is an Olivier-nominated director of theatre, opera and film. At the age of twenty-six, she became the co-Artistic Director of the Gate Theatre in London's Notting Hill alongside Natalie Abrahami. During their tenure the tiny, above-pub theatre became a powerhouse of new writing, adaptations of classics and contemporary dance theatre. After leaving the Gate in 2012, she became an associate director at the Young Vic and Royal Court. Her work includes a visionary staging of *A Doll's House* (2012) in a version by Simon Stephens and starring Hattie Morahan, which transferred to the West End, a double bill of *Sea Wall/A Life* (2019), starring Jake Gyllenhaal on Broadway, and two critically acclaimed collaborations with Helen McCrory, *Medea* (2014) and *The Deep Blue Sea* (2016).

*'Helen McCrory walked in and said:
"I think Medea should be brushing her
teeth when she walks on stage".'*

When you were co-Artistic Director of the Gate Theatre in Notting Hill from 2007 to 2012, the theatre became known for, among other things, programming punchy new adaptations of canonical plays by young, contemporary playwrights – many of which you directed yourself. What inspired this desire to revisit the canon and remix it for the Gate?

I think when you're developing your practice as a young or emerging director you both need to develop your own, muscular directing style but also find your own voice. You need to try to discover your identity as an artist and that can be pretty challenging. Natalie Abrahami, my co-Artistic Director at the Gate, and I had a strong interest in creating new work and devising new pieces. But we also both felt there was something incredibly nourishing and deepening about working on great plays that have a very strong structure, incredible characterisation and a real depth of emotional landscape. Working on these types of plays as an early career director enables you to flex your own muscles and find your own voice, but in response to something that gives you an enormous amount back. And I think that was what we both found very exciting.

One of the things I loved directing at the Gate was a new version of Ibsen's *Hedda Gabler* by Lucy Kirkwood. It was thrilling to be able to work on a play that has such a robust and deep identity, and to be able to find my own voice in relation to that. The thing I loved then, and still love now, is being able to work on plays with complex psychology and lots of subtext. And, of course, Ibsen has that in spades. One of the things Natalie and I were trying to do with our programming was offer young or younger artists the opportunity to work on those kinds of plays so they could discover themselves in relation to other great artists, which I think can be a really galvanising way to work.

When you commissioned writers to create these new versions of canonical plays, were you seeking radical rewrites, or were you hoping the new versions would emphasise and hinge on the timeless, essential qualities of the originals? Or, indeed, something else entirely?

Translation and adaptation is a fascinating and complex area of theatre practice. Personally, I tend to approach the subject on a project-by-project basis, in that sometimes a classic play feels so connected to the now and so in sync with a contemporary audience that almost all it needs is clarifying and sort of enlivening by a thoroughly good translation. Whereas at other points, it feels exciting to adapt the text and find a deeper connection, either with another moment in history or with the now. At the Gate, we were always very excited to work with writers who would bring their own lens to the play and find a way to make sense of it through their own perspectives and interests.

When you approached playwrights with the seed ideas for these commissions, what response did you generally receive?

People were thrilled because in the same way that it's exciting for an emerging director to work on a great play, it's also really good practice for emerging *writers* to work on great plays. Many of the playwrights I've worked with, such as Polly Stenham, Simon Stephens, Lucy Kirkwood and Nick Payne, have also done adaptations of classic plays for me. Living in the dramaturgical DNA of a classic play is a very interesting thing to do as a dramatist. Something from that process imprints on you in the way you think about, for example, dramatic action, which means it's a pretty exciting space for an emerging writer to exist in. It's also a kind of release because one of the most frightening things about making anything is having an original idea and seeing that through. Whereas bathing in somebody else's brilliance and somebody else's ideas for a moment and responding to that – in a way becoming a secondary artist, rather than a primary artist – can be very releasing and creative.

When you're directing a work like, for example, Lucy Kirkwood's version of a Henrik Ibsen play, where does your own vision as the director factor into the equation? Do you feel like you're creating Carrie Cracknell's version of Ibsen or is it something closer to Carrie's version of Lucy's version of…?

There's a three-way marriage at work in the process because, as a director, you spend an enormous amount of time with the writer working on the adaptation. Which means, to some extent, the adaptation becomes an expression of your production interests. And that collaboration is often very meaningful. It also means you're then working on a text that's come to life through the director's vision. Ultimately, it becomes a very active and exciting collaboration between two contemporary theatre artists (director and playwright) over a great piece of material, which is like the lifeboat that you set off on. And it gives you both the opportunity to work in microcosmic detail together on how you want to bring that play to life.

As a rule, do you tend to work very closely with playwrights on this kind of new text?

Yes, I think that sort of detailed dramaturgical support on new plays and adaptations is one of the most important parts of the director's role. It's a place where you can encourage a writer to do their best work, and hopefully bring clarity and a directorial vision to the way the text evolves. If you do that well, that's when you get a really holistic form of theatre-making. That not only feels exciting but means the writer and the director are in lockstep moving towards the same kind of artistic expression.

Of the playwrights you've worked with over the years, what's specifically excited you about certain writers and the texts they created with you?

When I worked with Lucy Kirkwood on *Hedda Gabler*, there was an inventiveness, a kind of granular playfulness and instinctive emotional depth to her writing. We were trying to make contemporary links between the original and its new setting in what was then contemporary Notting Hill. So, for example, in Ibsen's play, the paper manuscript gets burnt, whereas in the updated version, Lucy decided to put it on a memory stick – which was a thing at the time. Her idea was that Hedda would break that open and eat the middle of the memory stick, and that was how she got rid of the book. That felt symbolic to me of how Lucy was trying to finely reimagine the material, which I found very enlivening.

Then, when I worked with Polly Stenham on *Julie* for the National Theatre in 2018, Polly essentially created a new play that was based on the structure of August Strindberg's original play, *Miss Julie*. To do so, she drew very deeply on her own experience and tried to evoke a world that felt absolutely contemporary and very particular. The result was a new play full of the chaos and sadness and anger and joy and privilege of a certain kind of North London house party. In bringing an enormous amount of herself to the text it again made for a very interesting relationship between the original material and the contemporary audience who were going to watch the new play.

In contrast, when I worked with Simon Stephens on Ibsen's *A Doll's House* for the Young Vic, and later for the West End, Simon and I both wanted to render up the play in a very subtle and psychologically detailed way but leave it in its own period. In a way, the decision we made together was that the play was kind of dramaturgically perfect and that the central conflicts might be diminished if we tried to bring it into the contemporary world. So, we decided to set it very much in the period Ibsen set it in, but tried to make the emotional, sexual undercurrents of the play as alive and fizzy as possible, which made for quite a different process of adaptation.

When you're working on an adaptation that is closer in style to Polly Stenham's *Julie* – meaning it is quite freely adapted from the original – how much do your conversations centre on the original

text? Do you find yourself returning quite frequently to the original or does the focus lie almost entirely in the new creation?

Each writer works differently. Often, they will read a section of the original play and then work on the adaptation from that. At the beginning, it tends to be very much rooted in the original. Then over time, as the new adaptation becomes more robust, our time and energy are spent improving that in a very granular way. Sometimes, you'll reach a stage where you'll read the whole of the new adaptation and then think: 'Right, it's time to go back and reread the original.' It's often useful when you can see there's a problem, like a fault line in the structure of the new piece, to go back and understand whether that's something you have created through adaptation, or whether it's a weakness in the original text.

But it completely depends. If it's a relatively faithful translation to a large extent, then you're working all the time from the new literal translation. If it's a fairly free new adaptation, then normally the original text becomes the jumping-off point, or the sort of springboard. It remains in the DNA of the new piece, but you can be released from it over time.

As a director, has your approach to working on classical and canonical texts changed over the course of your career? Are you now coming to this sort of project with a different approach than you used to?

Not enormously, no. I always start a project with a huge amount of visual imagery and a very strong impulse about the people I want to work with on it. This often includes members of the design team, the writer and sometimes a specific actor. Once that team is established, we all start to build a relationship with the text where all these different ideas and instincts feed into establishing the world of the play we are making.

When you're working on a classic that has been performed, in some cases, for generations, and has potentially received now-iconic or

very famous productions, does the production history of the work weigh heavily on you?

Yes, always. In fact, there are definitely some classics I wouldn't touch because they've been so brilliantly realised in recent theatre history. Past productions can have a complicated impact on the development of each new piece. When I was working on *A Doll's House* with the brilliant designer Ian MacNeil, we kept trying to think about what the traditional baggage the play carried with it was, and what the traditional ways of staging it involved. And although the production choices we made were not particularly radical aesthetically, we found it helpful to try to keep saying: 'The clichéd version of this moment would be *x*', and then we would deliberately put that idea or concept in the bin, as it were, and instead try to find our own moment, our own motif, our own image, and our own idea.

When you're working on classics, you're working on them in response to their own performance history, and how you navigate that is a big part of the challenge of working on those texts and bringing them up to date. I watch as many earlier productions of the plays that I'm working on as I can, because you always learn things from other people's impulses and interpretations. It's also a helpful way of learning where there might be, for example, structural fault lines in the play, as these are normally revealed again and again by watching other people's adaptations or productions, which then – hopefully – helps you to circumnavigate those issues in the text.

Is something similar true for actors who are taking on those big, classic roles we find in canonical plays? Do you find, for instance, that actors sometimes arrive at the rehearsal room with pre-existing assumptions, ideas or beliefs about a certain character or storyline?

Yes, I think this is particularly the case with great classic roles. Actors walk into the rehearsal space with terrifying baggage about how the roles have been performed before. Part of the role of the director in that moment is to actively work with the company to find your own taste and sensibility in how you want to render those characters, and to encourage the actors to put that baggage away and think for themselves as much as possible.

All great actors want nothing more than to find an original way in. Actually, if all of their concentration and focus is on them as an actor meeting the character in a genuine way, then they will find something new. Working with Helen McCrory on *Medea* at the National Theatre in 2014 was extraordinary because she had such iconoclastic ideas about how to play that character, which were completely enlivening and influenced the whole production. On day one, she walked in and said, 'I think Medea should be brushing her teeth when she walks on stage.' And it just set the whole tone for everybody. Because then we were thinking about how to find a truthfulness and a realness in these characters, rather than keeping them as archetypes, which Greek characters can feel like in those epic plays. Similarly, when Michaela Coel came to play the nurse in *Medea*, she didn't have a clear route in at the beginning. So, I kept saying to her, 'Bring your self, Michaela, your self is extraordinary.' The question I was really asking was: 'What happens if you really meet that character on stage?' And she did. Having the actors working in that way on these kinds of parts empowers the entire company to find their own route through.

Is it often the case that an actor, like you describe Helen McCrory doing with Medea, will end up shaping an individual character so much they also end up heavily influencing the feeling of the entire staging?

Of course. Great actors like Helen McCrory have limitless imagination and this instinctive understanding of the character they're playing. That's what's so beautiful about directing because when you're preparing the production pre-rehearsal, you're thinking about an entire world, which you're trying to evoke through image, idea, text, music. But then as soon as the actors arrive, they see the play through the perspective of their own characters and, suddenly, the detail and the complexity becomes infinite. The best productions I've worked on have always had the identities of the actor indelibly stamped on them.

When you're in the rehearsal room with those actors, what do your conversations typically focus on together?

I try to keep talking as much as possible about the conditions of the world the characters are in, and what they're doing to each other. We also talk a lot about the backstory of the characters and the history of their relationships. Other than that, I try to minimise bigger, more generalised conversations about what the play is and what it represents or means. Of course, some of our time has to be spent doing that, and we have to understand the context of what we're making and where it sits, but I try to focus the rehearsal time as much as possible on the act of doing and the act of being.

Do those rehearsal-room conversations ever hit on the personal experiences of the actors in the room and how that connects with their characters?

We talk an enormous amount about lived experience in rehearsal. I talk a lot about my own lived experience, and I'm interested in an actor's connection to the concerns of their characters. For me, everything that is interesting in drama is psychology, and so trying to use experiences from life to understand the psychological impulses of a character is the core of the work, in a way. However, I do try to encourage actors not to use incredibly raw, unresolved life trauma in rehearsal. I don't think it's safe or massively appropriate. Which means that if we were going to use emotional history to inform the work that we were doing, we would try to find events or experiences that felt somewhat resolved for the performer. But of course, we don't know what a performer is thinking about or even doing, ultimately, when they're on stage. One of the many things that was extraordinary about working with Helen McCrory was the sense I had of the very wild and dark exploration she was doing night to night to bring to her character. That kind of exploration will forever remain a mystery to everyone apart from the actor themselves, and is one of the things that makes a great rendering of a character feel complex, mysterious, unknowable and, most of all, compelling.

What does it give you, as a director, to work with an actor like her?

Everything. I'm so lucky to have worked with such wonderful actors because when you work with wonderful actors they offer you and the play their instincts, thoughts, feelings and renditions of particular moments. Thanks to that, the work becomes about encouraging that level of investigation in detail. When that happens, the task of the director becomes editorial. Rather than starting each day trying to generate ideas from yourself, the task shifts to become a very acute form of listening, and observing and encouraging. That's innately more creative because something's being generated by the actor in the moment and you're there supporting and shaping that. It's a really thrilling feeling.

Are there any specific ways that working with great actors has altered your process or methods of working in the rehearsal room?

When I worked with Jake Gyllenhaal on Nick Payne's *A Life*, I realised that because of his history as a film actor, he was less interested in working with as much structure or planning as I normally would. It was actually fascinating for me to let go of some of that structure and instead operate in response to Gyllenhaal's instinctive understanding, moment to moment. I learnt an enormous amount during that process, because it was a different way into a play than I would normally take. I had to also accept that what he would do each night would be very different to the one before and the one after it, but that it was always a version of his truth and it always felt very connected.

The whole experience was fascinating because it upended a lot of the beliefs I had about my role as a director and my relationship to acting. When you work with actors who have enormous identities in their own right, you tend to come out of the process slightly changed. But when you go into the next process with a different actor you need to respond to them in the way they need to be responded to. As I'm getting older, I think my process is more fluid because I'm responding more actively to who, and what, is happening in the room.

Nadia Fall

Theatre and therapy

Nadia Fall is the Artistic Director of Theatre Royal Stratford East. A playwright and director, she has created work for theatre, television and film. Before leading Stratford East, she was an associate director at the National Theatre. Her productions there include Michaela Coel's electric *Chewing Gum Dreams* (2014), and Inua Ellams' affecting *Three Sisters* (2020), which relocated Chekhov's story to 1960s Nigeria. She has also created work for the Bridge Theatre, Bush Theatre, Regent's Park Open Air Theatre and the Lyric Hammersmith.

'When you step inside the rehearsal room, you're stepping inside this very intense space.'

In an article for *The Stage* in January 2021, you wrote that, 'Theatre is by its very definition a congregation of people, engaging us in the act of empathy. I believe it's the cheapest and most effective form of group therapy there is.' I thought that would be a nice jumping-off point for talking about your practice and what you do. So, to start with – why is theatre like group therapy?

Scientists have looked into the physiological things that happen in a theatre, like heartbeats synchronising – those of the audience with those of the players on stage – which I think is so profound. We sit in the dark, and although you might not have particularly noticed on your way in who the other members of the audience are, in the dark you become one powerful entity. And when we see live storytelling, characters going through whatever the given struggle is in that particular story, we very naturally project our own lives and struggles onto what we are seeing. Whether the play mirrors our own lives or very different ones – theatre engages us in the act of empathy through which we get the gift of sensing we're not alone.

And I think that's the ultimate human struggle, the feeling of loneliness and being alone, and that occasional insurmountable feeling of alienation. It's the human condition. So yes, I think that when you're sitting together as an audience and watching stories on stage as a shared experience, something about that makes you feel less lonely because you become aware, at least on a subconscious level, that we all struggle, but we're all in it together.

Do you think that is something that's unique to theatre rather than other art forms?

Yes. Though all art has its merit, and we need the different forms because, sometimes, watching a film is perfect, whereas other times it just doesn't hit the spot. Sometimes, you need to go and dance at a live concert. But I think what's unique about theatre is that, and all of us who work in the industry know this, it's got this profound therapeutic quality. It's ancient and it doesn't matter what culture or country you go to, there's a form of theatre going on. Theatre is part of our human existence, it's storytelling in one form or another, so it won't go away, even in very difficult times.

Does that understanding of it inform how you make work?

I don't think it's a conscious, intellectual part of what I do. But I do know that, as an artist, when I read a play and become interested in directing it, that's because something in that story feels true, and by 'true' I mean that I recognise that human thing in it.

As audience members, we all recognise when something doesn't feel true or truthful. This doesn't mean the play has to be a work of naturalism or a 'kitchen-sink drama'; theatre that is very abstract or absurdist can feel true. It's dependent on whether the artist has managed to manifest life and the human condition authentically. But when we sit down in a theatre and feel something isn't truthful, we clench up and get a bit uncomfortable, because we're all experts in the human condition and we can kind of smell if something isn't quite true.

And does it also feed into the programming decisions you make as the Artistic Director at Stratford East?

Definitely. Everyone has their own affinities and styles of storytelling, but as an artistic director the sweet spot is all about having a real breadth of work represented. I want different types of stories and different storytellers from different backgrounds, whether that's being from different countries or different ethnicities, ages, or whatever. Basically, I'm trying to get variety because variety is dynamic and rich.

At Stratford East, we've historically had quite a strong political stance, which I try to reflect in the programming, along with simply trying to commission all the people I rate as directors, playwrights, actors, and creatives. In a way, we're trying to create the perfect storm with each production and each season but there are always things against us – like money! Some plays call for a really big cast or complicated scenography and that costs more to put on. Another factor is getting the rights for plays. This seems to be changing but, to many people, there's still a kudos attached to being in the West End or on the South Bank or wherever and, of course, we sit outside of that. So sometimes, particularly if you're approaching someone from abroad, you have to try to convince agents, rights holders, and artists that this is the place where their play should be on. None of this is insurmountable, they're the parameters you work within and the obvious challenges you face as an artistic director. We're also constricted by the amount we can produce each year, and it's harder to get your vision for a theatre across to audiences if you're only able to produce three or four things a year, with the rest having to be touring shows. I mean, with touring shows you're still very picky and only select the ones that fit with what you want to be on the stage at your theatre, but it's a bit trickier because, obviously, you can't note a touring show or have deep, detailed conversations with a director about the work. And, of course, to an audience, whether something is produced at home or is touring doesn't matter, what they see is just a show on at your theatre and they expect it to be of a certain quality.

It's very challenging, but I remember David Lan saying to me years ago that when he first started as Artistic Director at the Young Vic they could only afford to produce one show of their own per year. But by the end of his tenure, look how prolific that theatre was! His message was that you've got to hang on in there and in time you'll earn the right – and be solvent enough – to produce more and get more people in to make work.

That sounds like a lot to fill your head with. Do you find it hard negotiating the balance between being an artistic director and an artist?

Headspace is challenging. But actually, I really, really love both aspects of the jobs. They overlap, but they are integrally different. The truth about being an artistic director is that the more solvent you are, the more scope you have. I'm not saying that money alone makes you a better artistic director, but it does mean you can express yourself more artistically. Working within tight parameters is the tough bit. There's all the unglamourous things like health and safety, and budgets and HR – which are a huge part of running a building.

I love it more than I thought I would. I love choosing the director to go with a play and helping them talk about it and cast it, and then being in read-throughs and noting the runs and, most of all, championing the team. It's like when a friend or family member does well, you get this immensely proud feeling. I find that really joyful and absolutely fantastic.

With my own work, I love creating it but I'm very self-critical. I'm always thinking that this could or that could have been better, and so I find it hard to genuinely celebrate it in the same way I do with other people's work that I've programmed as an AD.

Going back to the 'theatre as therapy' theme, do you find the act of making your own work therapeutic, despite being very critical of it?

I do. When you step inside the rehearsal room, you're stepping inside this very intense space where you might be encountering characters with histories that overlap with your own traumatic incidents, and that can be quite difficult. I think this comes from my background in making participatory theatre, but I'm extremely careful about how I talk about 'theatre' and 'therapy', because although I believe rehearsing and making theatre can be therapeutic – it isn't therapy. I'm not qualified to be a therapist and the rehearsal space is not group therapy, it's a place of work where we've often got three or four weeks – in the rehearsal space – to make a piece of theatre and open a show.

But there are, of course, moments when you're talking about or working on tough stuff which can be enormously challenging. I've tried to address this in some way at Stratford East by signing up to a counselling service that anyone can access to talk through and process emotionally and psychologically taxing stuff brought up when working on a play. It's also there for our team to access to support them through the process. It's an anonymous resource there if people need it. Nowadays, we're much more aware of mental health whereas, in the past, I think there were times when creatives and actors were encouraged to open their hearts – but there was nobody available to teach them to how to pack it all back up again after they'd accessed the pain and trauma.

But in terms of the therapeutic value of making theatre, I've certainly found that in the toughest moments of my life, once you step inside the rehearsal room it calls for such complete concentration that everything else kind of disappears for those hours. I think it's also because everything that happens in the rehearsal room forces you to work in the present and be completely present. I tell young directors that you can do all the prep you want, but there's nothing that beats getting a good night's sleep and arriving at the room fully engaged – like absolutely in the moment. I don't do meditation or mindfulness or any of those things, but I guess this is my version of being fully in the present.

You mentioned working within participatory theatre. Do you think there are some types of theatre – whether that's community theatre or verbatim theatre or theatre-in-the-round or theatre outdoors – where the therapeutic value is particularly pronounced?

I honestly think it can be absolutely anything. Because you never know what story in what form is going to connect with someone – you can't call it. I think if something is very abstract and cerebral, then maybe a completely first-time audience might find it off-putting. But even that is a bit of a British thing. When you go to Europe, young people are much more open to abstract thought and to things that aren't linear or literal. But if we look at visual art, people come in droves to the Tate Modern and they're not asking, 'What does it mean?' any more. They're up for having an immersive experience.

I think we're a bit obsessed in theatre with analysing our audiences, which comes from a good place because we're trying to grow our audiences and develop a diverse audience, and we're trying to reach different communities and ages. However, with that focus can come a slightly reductive and presumptuous idea of what audiences want and need. If we could get young people to watch a wide breadth of work, in different styles and genres, we would open up such incredible possibilities for them, for their imaginations and their thinking. Imagine investing in such culturally rich audiences of the future.

When I've worked with young people, I've used such a wide variety of material, from a Lorca play to rap and spoken word, and it would be hugely limiting to think that young people living in inner-city London, for example, are only interested in the rap and exploring issues that are part of their own lived experiences. Though that is of course valid, it's about moving beyond that for me. However, we're getting further and further from that as the arts are being steadily eradicated from the state education system.

Lots of people have presumptions about what an audience is and what they are like, but those views are very rarely entirely accurate. I remember when we did Conor McPherson's *Shining City* at Stratford East in 2021, and a couple of people said to me: 'Is that a very Stratford East play?' and I replied, 'What do you mean by that?' I mean, it's a play where a group of people tell you about their life and their pains. They're working class – if you want to know that – and certain characters are struggling financially or struggling with trauma. And it's by a brilliant, very celebrated playwright, and performed by a brilliant bunch of actors. What, precisely, then, isn't 'Stratford East' about it? I think we need to challenge these kinds of assumptions.

Do you think equally hard about your audience when you're making your own work?

I try to. It is my responsibility to be an outside eye looking at a piece of theatre from the perspective of the audience and keeping vigilant to ensure all elements are as sharp as they could be. Part of that is trying to guess how an audience is going to feel at a particular moment and whether they will need more or less of something. I know there's never going to be a 'one size fits all' solution because we've all got different tastes and experiences, but I'm trying to make sure an audience feels as connected as possible to the joke or the pathos within a story.

This, really, is why previews are so important. When I'm sitting in an auditorium full of people, they're telling me how they feel about the play. And they do that through things like showing me when they laugh or when they start fidgeting or when they cough or get up to go to the loo. It's my job to take this information and mould the play in response to that. Obviously, nobody is going to like everything, and you can't keep everyone happy. In fact, if you're trying to make everyone like something you're not focusing on the story enough.

It's a hard balance to strike because directors are control freaks! We're trying to control the story and tell it in a certain way. But the thing about theatre is that so much is out of one's control. It's not like writing a novel, where you can control all the words, or a film where you can edit what you don't want after the fact. Theatre is an unwieldy beast where, ultimately, you're collaborating with all the other creatives and performers, who all also bring their own interpretations and input to the storytelling.

Sticking with previews – are you someone who will make big changes during previews?

I'm not as brave as some. I think it all depends on how many previews you have and, more importantly, the appetite and ability within the company for late changes. When you're working on new plays, it's more normal to make big changes right up until opening night – sometimes cutting whole scenes or half an hour off the running time. But even if they're prepared to go with it, that's tough on the actors, because some can learn new lines overnight and some can't. Occasionally, this means you're faced with a decision where you know it would be good for the play to make a major change but if you did so, the actors would lose their confidence, their lines, their blocking, and everything would fall like a house of cards.

So, you have to be very careful when making those decisions. I've worked as an assistant and associate to other directors who I have witnessed being incredibly brave with how much they cut and change at the eleventh hour. I am less keen because I find the need for the company to have repetition, and through this gain a confidence in their work, outweighs the need for cuts or changes to text.

The stakes around taking risks also feel so high nowadays. In the theatre in the UK, you're often working to a specific schedule, you might start with a workshop – if you're lucky – followed by auditions, rehearsal, tech and, eventually, press night. And, in truth, you're worried about reviews and sales, and sometimes you're so petrified of something going wrong you don't dare veer away from the traditional process. Yet, ironically, the best work comes out of risk.

Does that sense of fear increase when you're directing at the theatre where you're also the Artistic Director? Do you feel a bigger sense of responsibility, in a way?

Probably a little bit more. As a director, you want everything you do to be good – to reflect the human condition, to inspire. And with our industry, it doesn't matter if you did a beautifully profound play three years ago, it's the one that you're doing right now that matters. I do feel a huge sense of responsibility. And that's a good thing, in many ways. Frankly, you've got to care deeply because, as the AD, the theatre is my home from home. I spend more time there than in my own home. I know everyone personally who has worked on a show, and I know the impact it has on individuals and a building when a show is doing well critically and at the box office.

So, of course, you feel a huge responsibility to make sure something you make at the theatre you also run is a success. But of course, I also care a lot about shows I do outside of the building. Every time you make a piece of work, you're sharing a piece of yourself with the world, and it matters every time. For example, when I directed *Three Sisters* at the National Theatre there was the artistic endeavour, but I also wanted the light from the show to reflect back on Stratford East. It's important to me that we're seen as part of any major conversation that is happening in the industry. I want Theatre Royal Stratford East to be a really important epicentre of great work by great artists.

Ola Ince

Building a visual world – and how to ask an actor to sound more like an egg

Ola Ince is an award-winning theatre, film and opera director. A former recipient of the prestigious Genesis Future Directors Award, she has created work for venues including the Young Vic, Donmar Warehouse, Royal Court and Shakespeare's Globe. Her bold and visually articulate approach to theatre has seen her work – much of which centres on the themes of race, gender and power structures – widely celebrated by audiences, critics and journalists. Her acclaimed productions include *Poet in Da Corner* (Royal Court, 2018 and 2020), *The Convert* (Young Vic, 2018) and *Romeo and Juliet* (Shakespeare's Globe, 2021).

'I'm reaching out into the works, pinpointing something and bringing it back.'

We've spoken a few times previously, on the first occasion about your production of Branden Jacobs-Jenkins' *Appropriate* **at the Donmar Warehouse in 2019 and, on the second occasion, about Aleshea Harris's** *Is God Is* **at the Royal Court in 2021. In both conversations, you described yourself as a very visual person. Could you start by explaining how being such a visual person impacts the type of theatre you make?**

Relatively recently, I realised that I think via images and see the world in snapshots. So when I'm making work, it's almost like I'm putting together a flipbook of pictures. I build a collection of images and then flesh them out, or I encourage other people to create images and then we flesh those images out into something that's moving, living and breathing. Right at the very start of my process, when I first encounter a play I've decided I want to direct, I create a visual mood board. That mood board probably speaks to my subconscious and the idea is that it will help me learn more about how I feel about the play – how it moves me, what it reminds me of, etc. – once I filter it through the imagery.

That sounds quite convoluted, but in practice it is simple. I read a play and the first thing I then do is grab *The Art Book*, which is basically a bumper collection of famous Western artworks from medieval times to now. I flick through it quite quickly and mark any image that reminds me of what I've just read. This results in about a hundred flagged images, which I'll then collect together and, firstly, try to figure out what, for example, a dustbin, an egg and a red flag have to do with the play. I'll then repeat the process with loads of different art books, and then distil down all these images I've marked until around twenty remain. And I trust those images somehow contain the essence of the play and help me communicate the production I want to make.

I then make a folder of those images and use it to help me select a creative team and talk to them about what we're trying to achieve. Everyone I have worked with so far has found that useful because although it sounds a bit random, it actually gives us tangible things to discuss and to try to unpick in relation to the production. So, for example, it could be an image of a child screaming down the lens of a camera and I'll explain how it was the boldness or the aggression of that image that spoke to me. Or it could be an image of an egg and I'll talk to them about how this egg has a very fragile quality but is also very ugly – and that's a mix I want to preserve in this production.

And every creative department sees that folder – the set designer, the costume designer, the lighting designer, sound design, music designer and so on – they all look at this image and we collectively figure out how to incorporate that feeling into the production. Like, how is this production going to sound like that egg? Or, how is the lighting going to make sure that egg is clearly ugly? It also means that we can all refer back to those original images if we're feeling a little lost and check in to see that it's all still building towards the same thing.

I also show those images to the playwright, which quickly gives them a sense of what the play has evoked for me. Some writers probably find it a bit strange, but it does mean that they're not surprised by what a production is looking like if they turn up to, say, a dress rehearsal or a technical rehearsal, because that visual language has been there all along. I should also add that it's not entirely visuals, I will also create playlists – because it's a bit obscure trying to sound 'like an egg'! – but that's basically how the process works and how I start it.

Does the process change from play to play?

Yes, slightly. When designer Fly Davis and I worked on Branden Jacobs-Jenkins' *Appropriate* at the Donmar Warehouse, I started off with the same process of assembling a collection of images, which helped us to establish the tone of the show. But at the same time, I was working as the International Associate Director on the musical *Tina*, which meant I got to travel a lot. One time, I was in New York on a trip to audition people and, in the middle of the night, I went to this amazing bookstore and found loads of fascinating books of photographs showing American plantations, like the kind *Appropriate* is set on, which were very useful. Then, when I returned to England, we managed to convince Michael Longhurst, the Artistic Director at the Donmar, that we should go on a research trip. We had to fight to get that trip funded and had to make this little package explaining where we would go, and why, and what the benefit to the show would be.

Brilliantly, he did fund it. And so, although the play is set in Arkansas, we went to New Orleans because in New Orleans there are a lot of well-preserved plantations that are used for films or for creating period pieces. We visited three plantations and took a huge number of photos. We also bought a lot of books on plantation architecture, and ended up combining that original folder of images with information from those books and the photos we took. The final set design, which Fly created, actually used authentic features from real-life plantations. I believe she copied the ceiling of one plantation and took the floor and staircase from another. I had known, right from the start, that I wanted this place to feel haunted. I had been looking at eerie images of zombies and stuff, so it was amazing to combine those references points with historically accurate, naturalistic ones as well.

The other thing we did while on the trip was record the cicadas, which became a big part of the final production. Knowing what those places look like, and even what they sound like, was invaluable – both to us and to the actors. You might think that going to the real-life location you're trying to recreate would spoil your imagination or restrict you, but it had the opposite effect. I felt like all the research made it easier to visualise things in detail and allowed my imagination to go further. I think if you're not having to think so hard about what a room will look like – because you know what those rooms look like – it means you can think about things like: 'What goes on beyond this room?' The images also help to keep things from getting too academic in the rehearsal room – which is never a good thing – and allow the actors to digest the work and turn it into living and breathing action.

On the occasions where you can't go on a research trip, do you do book-based research or other forms of research instead?

Yes – and just to be clear, I've only ever been able to convince one person to send me on a research trip, and no one has offered to send me on one since! My materials, ordinarily, are books. Even on that research trip, I bought lots of books. I love reading and, while I don't want a rehearsal room to become overly academic, I don't mind being academic on my own.

Saying that, I have on several occasions brought in lecturers to the rehearsal room who have spoken on topics like, for example, what it means to be Jewish in America today, and so on. I find that's a good way of being a bit academic while not throwing a book at someone. Having a lecturer run a workshop, rather than giving a lecture, allows actors to try things out and play around a bit and do something that's a bit more kinetic than sitting there and listening.

Going back to my own research, I also watch a lot of films and documentaries, and listen to music. With *Appropriate*, I watched a lot of films to help me understand what Arkansas is like or could be like. Watching films for this purpose also makes you aware of how potent art can be, because it can be tempting to regurgitate stories or references or images without checking how factually accurate they are. Just because someone else has included them in a film about a place, doesn't mean it's necessarily the truth!

How important do you think it is to be factually accurate when creating an aesthetic for a play?

It depends on what it is. For example, *Dutchman* by Amiri Baraka – which I directed at the Young Vic in 2016 – was written in the 1960s and set in the 1960s. But my production was quite expressionistic. It was important the actors knew the historical truth of their characters, but it wasn't so important that the set design showed, for instance, an exact recreation of a 1960s subway. What mattered was creating feelings of danger, excitement and lust. Equally, with Anna Deavere Smith's *Twilight: Los Angeles, 1992* – which I worked on at the Gate Theatre in 2018 – it wasn't important to create a set that was exactly like LA in the 1990s, because even though that is an historical play it was, again, more important to communicate the facts and the feelings of the piece.

But then with *Appropriate*, it was important to have an historically accurate set because the whole point of the play is to explore how racism still exists and is in our DNA. You can't muddy the timelines and the history, or that point would become unclear. So it varies depending on the play itself and what you're trying to communicate with the production.

Going back to that original folder of images – how much does the final show end up staying true to those pictures? Or, put another way, if you had to compile a folder of images at the end of a rehearsal period, do you think those images would be the same ones as you originally selected or would they have changed substantially?

I think some would go and some would stay. Once the creative team has been assembled and the set has been made, I don't usually refer back to those images again. They might be in the room, but I very rarely look at them. If I get a bit stuck or we need inspiration, I sometimes check in with them, but not very often. In many ways, it would be worrying if everything was exactly as I imagined in the first place when we got to the end of the creation period. I would be very concerned if nothing has evolved.

Usually, when I look back at a show, I can see that certain initial ideas are still very clearly present, and others have been totally replaced. I would estimate that around 20% of the original images end up being present in the final show in some form or another – not necessarily in a way that someone outside of the production would be able to detect, but in a way that I can still see. I'm never completely wedded to the images and I'm not like: 'Everyone stop! That image is no longer clear!' I just use them as ideas or guidelines.

You also mentioned creating playlists. Do you use those to create a certain mood or environment in the rehearsal space, or are they resources that you take to the sound designer or composer, and

present them with as the basis for the music and sound in the production?

It's usually a bit like the folder of images, where it's about creating and sharing a tone, rather than the exact music. I normally share it with everyone in the creative team, not just the sound team, because music and imagery both evoke so much for me, so it's the clearest way of expressing what I'm searching for. Then, if we've agreed that one or two of those tracks are particularly useful, I might also share them with the actors, maybe just as part of the first-day meet-and-greet to help them understand the essence of the thing we're aiming at.

Not everyone finds this very helpful, but some actors love creating their own playlists as a way of exploring who their character is and so they can say, 'I think my character would listen to this...', and sometimes I totally agree and sometimes I intervene and say, 'Actually I think it would be more like *this*...' It's similar to when I've had actors go shopping for their characters. I'll ask them to go on ASOS and show me what they think they would wear or like.

Most of the time, the music the actors pick is part of an exercise in getting to know their characters and acts as a stepping-stone to understanding the play better. But when we were working on Danai Gurira's *The Convert* at the Young Vic in 2018, the cast shared lots of music during the rehearsal period, and lots of it ended up appearing in the final show. That was great, because it made them feel like it was their show because they had contributed to it in so many ways.

Where does the text fit into all of this? Specifically, does this mean that you're not a director who would, for example, start a rehearsal period sitting at the table and doing a deep-dive into a script?

Well, despite all we've talked about, I would still describe myself as a director who is interested in the script itself – and I do start with table work! I use those collected images to help me communicate a feeling or an aesthetic or a vibe. It's also about creating a vision, which some directors would spend an hour talking about to their team, whereas I say, 'Everyone, look at this picture.' But, in general, when we're in the rehearsal room, we are not spending hours poring over the pictures – we're spending hours dissecting the text! Otherwise, the pictures are too abstract.

I do very conventional things like: facts and questions, where we note down the things we know for sure from the script and then interrogate it. I also unit the text and, increasingly, I action it. Which means we do also do table work. However, I try to keep activities mixed up a bit, even if we are spending the first week – or even first two weeks – doing table work. I don't want anyone to end up feeling like a couch potato. We might, for example, do table work followed by a couple of hours with the movement director. Or table work followed by a session with the vocal coach.

I find that without facts and questions, people will get lost. It all becomes about how someone feels, rather than what we know to be true from the text. If the text says it is a Sunday, that is a fact regardless of whether someone feels it is a Saturday. Or, if someone feels like their character would do something, it's worth asking: 'Why?' And, crucially, 'Where does it say that in the text?' We want to explode everything, but not just for the sake of it. It needs to be done with real precision and we need to know that we're making choices that are fully informed.

I always say to people, 'I don't mind if we're going to set this play underwater or make this character an elephant, but until we analyse the text and see what the playwright intended, we don't know whether that character was an elephant all along and we won't have actually done anything subversive by making them one. We need to see what's in the text and then decide whether to subvert it or not.'

That's how my brain works. Those images and track lists I've been talking about might sound wild and wacky and random, but ultimately they have come from the text. I have to hope I've read the text well enough to understand what it is asking for. In a way, I'm reaching out into the work, pinpointing something and bringing it back so I can better communicate with the actors and make sure we're all seeing the same thing. So, when I do ask someone to be a bit more like that weird egg when saying that line, everyone understands exactly what I mean by that!

Katie Mitchell

Towards a bicycle-powered future of theatre

Katie Mitchell is a prolific international director of theatre and opera in the UK and across Europe, who has directed over one hundred productions. One of the most important and influential directors to work in British theatre over the past thirty years, she is known for her pioneering 'live cinema' work, where actors on stage are simultaneously filmed, allowing the audience to watch both the live performance and the filmed action. In Mitchell's productions, the use of filming offers a uniquely female perspective on the story taking place. More recently, she has focused on sustainable methods of making theatre; for example, using onstage bicycles to generate the electricity needed to power a show. She has written a seminal book on directing, *The Director's Craft*.

'Theatre needs to have a conversation with the reality of climate change.'

Your book, *The Director's Craft*, has become one of the definitive texts on how to work in a rehearsal room. Since it was published in 2008, has your approach to directing changed in any significant way?

I still use the basic principles outlined in the book when I direct, although I have distilled them further into the six simple layers: time, place, character biography, immediate circumstances, events and intentions. I have stopped using some elements described in the book, like improvisation, practical work on the ideas underpinning the text and the analysis of relationships. My approach to directing has also been changed by working in Germany where I have learnt much more about concept – an aspect of directing I do not write about in the book. Furthermore, my view of directing now encompasses a more complete understanding of the balance of the administrative and artistic functions of the role.

You shared that you are working on a revised edition of the book. How do you plan to explore and expand on those things in the new version?

In the new version of *The Director's Craft,* I will be trimming out the aspects of practice that I no longer use and organising the book more strongly around the six simple layers – how they are used from pre-rehearsal preparation to the finished staging. The new version will also reference a wider spectrum of plays instead of one classical playtext, allowing the readers to apply the techniques described to different texts. Concept and how the administrative side of the job works alongside the artistic will be explored in a second book with the working title, *The Essential Guide to Theatre Directing*. When I wrote the first book, it was at the end of twenty years of working inside British text-based practice, and my productions reflected the influence of naturalism and Stanislavsky on me, and the practices being applied in British theatre. Soon after writing it, I started working extensively in Europe and in opera, both of which invited me into other aspects of directing, like concept. Working in Europe has made me realise how UK theatre makes assumptions about the function of the director that contradict how the role is executed and perceived outside the UK. Traditionally, Britain has encouraged the mode of theatre-making where the director executes the writer's intentions, whereas in Germany, for example, theatres and audiences are more interested in the director's interpretation or concept. The second book will unfold the practical lessons about directing that I learnt working in Europe.

Why is it important to write about the administrative aspects of the job?

When I started working as a director, I was very focused on the artistic side of theatre directing: how to work with actors, with set design, with lighting, with sound, with music, etc. I wasn't as aware of the administrative functions, like how to work with marketing, press or how to manage budgets or schedules. Because I was fixated on perfecting the artistic side of things, I didn't realise that I needed to develop soft skills like time management, money management and communication for the administrative aspects of the job happening outside the rehearsal room. The more work I've done, particularly outside of the UK and on a very large scale, the more I've realised that 60% of my time is spent on the administrative function of my job and 40% is spent working on artistic choices. Sometimes that ratio is more like 70:30. I've come to see how important the administrative side of the job is and how it enhances the artistic outcomes. This discovery is something I've prioritised in the new book, so that a younger generation of theatre-makers don't have to go on the somewhat roundabout journey I took to get the administrative skills right.

Has the success of *The Director's Craft* led to people turning up to work with you with a specific idea of what they think 'working with Katie Mitchell' is going to be like and, if so, has that been a good or a bad thing?

Sometimes the people I'm working with have read the book, and sometimes not. If they have read it, it is never a bad thing. It means we have a bit of shared territory from which we can start to make something. But it's certainly not a prerequisite for any working relationship, and sometimes reading the book can backfire because I do use some tools from the book differently now to how I did when I wrote about them fourteen years ago. My students at Royal Holloway, where I'm a professor on the MA Theatre Directing course, are very good at pointing out these inconsistencies! In fact, this confusion in a teaching setting (between the book and my living practice) is a major reason for rewriting the book.

Do you like the writing and, in this case, rewriting process? By which I mean, is it helpful in clarifying aspects of your own practice?

Yes. The process of writing always makes me more conscious of my practice and helps me get better at directing. It allows me to think about what I do, both in terms of my own work and what's going on beyond it. I spend a lot of time reflecting on what performance is, what theatre is, why we make it and how we communicate our ideas. The act of writing forces me to follow through my reflections and articulate them simply and clearly. Often it exposes unclear links or connections where I have missed out a step in what I do practically. Directing in a rehearsal room is a very intense experience where the director is constantly on the spot to deliver ideas or give feedback or lead groups towards shared goals. This pressure is intensified by the short length of rehearsals. This means that directors can cut corners or take short cuts in their work. Writing removes the pressure of the rehearsal room and allows the thought processes more space and time – you can, for example, spend an hour reflecting on a tiny loose connection in a sequence of practical exercises and come up with a better link or step.

Has working with younger people through your teaching made you recalibrate or re-evaluate your own work?

Of course. I've particularly enjoyed the way my students teach me back, inviting me to think in a different way about subjects like feminism, gender identity, racism or ecology – and intersectionality. I have taught at Royal Holloway for several years, but it was during lockdown (when I chose to fill my time with teaching young people) that I learnt the most from the young people I worked with. I taught young people virtually in schools, universities, drama schools and workshop settings across the UK and Europe. This process revealed how my practice had developed shorthand inaccuracies which the students helped me resolve. They also invited me into the complexity of contemporary identity politics and deepened my understanding of issues like neurodiversity, ethnicity, and access. These exchanges modulated and enriched my practice considerably, running alongside discoveries I made bringing up a teenaged daughter.

How has your interest in ecology and the state of the planet informed your working and artistic practices?

I started making productions about climate change in 2012 after meeting a scientist who – Cassandra-like – forecast all the issues we are now facing, like mass migration, food and water supply concerns, extreme weather events and so on. Since then, I have made nine productions, including performance lectures with scientists, bike-powered off-grid performance text and music events (where the performers power the electricity) and latterly, a new system for international touring where no people or materials move between venues. Until relatively recently, I could choose whether I wanted to make a show about the environmental catastrophe or not. Now, as climate change so clearly envelops us (with recent wildfires and flooding in Europe being two of many global catastrophes), there is no longer any choice. All our practice in theatre needs to have a conversation with the reality of climate change, in terms of the content of productions, their form, and the ways we source, use, and build any materials we use. I've found it relatively easy to make my practice more sustainable in a practical way; it's the content of the shows and the performance form that I find more challenging. Climate change is such an enormous subject to attempt to represent on stage and I often end up with a production that is not theatrically interesting. Last year I directed Chekhov's *The Cherry Orchard* from the point of view of the trees, backgrounding the human beings (who were in a sound-sealed box acting the lines but mostly inaudible) and foregrounding filmed footage of a cherry orchard across the four seasons. Like many productions in this area, I found that by changing one element (backgrounding humans), I ended up replacing it with another (foregrounding the more-than-human) but not finding a way of making that new foregrounded element theatrical or interesting to watch. In the end trying to tackle climate change has altered my practice by making me much more aware of where materials come from and what their legacy should be. In terms of finding content and experimenting with form, I suppose you could say that the subject of climate change poses my practice with its most intractable and impossible challenge. But at least I'm not alone with that challenge. The planetary emergency is inviting everyone in the artistic community to step up and respond creatively. We need to model new systems of making shows and realise that this is not just an environmental issue, it's a question of social justice as well. It's a pretty challenging time to be an artist, but if we can step up and face this existential crisis, we will all probably be able to help a bit.

Are there also more practical ways in which your work has been shaped in response to the ecological crisis?

In responding to the ecological crisis, I've found myself creating off-grid bike-powered productions, thereby generating ways of performing plays that I never would have thought about before. The first show like this was Duncan Macmillan's *Lungs*, which I directed ten years ago at the Schaubühne in Berlin. The play is about a young cis couple working out whether to have a baby or not in the light of the climate crisis. In my production the two actors rode stationary bikes powering the electricity to light their faces whilst acting the text into microphones mounted on their handlebars. There were four other cyclists powering the sound system and a projected algorithm showing how many babies were born globally during the seventy-three minutes of the show. All the materials used were recycled, including the front curtain and clothing. Since then, I've directed three more bike-powered performances, including the first ever bike-powered classical concert, premiering Laura Bowler's *Houses Slide* at the Royal Festival Hall. I've become a great advocate for theatrical events which are off-grid, where we watch the artistic product whilst also experiencing the effort required to generate the electricity or sound or video, which is part of that product. Even when I'm not doing a production with bike power, I now always ask the people I'm working with about how we can make things in a more sustainable way, thinking both of where we source materials from and their legacy after the production is over. I used to be a real stickler for super-detailed scenography but now I'm much more open to making artistic compromises in response to issues relating to the sustainability of any of the materials or practical processes involved in making a production.

When I was first setting out to write this book, I toyed with the idea of consciously never asking any of the female directors interviewed a question about feminism or gender on the basis that 'a male director would never be asked what it is to reflect on being a man' and because, in my experience, many female artists find questions about femaleness deeply annoying...

When I was young, I felt just like that. I wanted theatre to be a meritocracy where I was measured by my work and where my gender was not a factor in how people looked at what I made or who I was. In interviews I never wanted to talk about my gender and if asked about it, I would become very irritated and say, 'Oh, why don't you ask Sam Mendes about what's it like to be a male director?' But the fact is, theatre is not a meritocracy. And the higher up you go, the clearer that is. Gender is often a feature of why women get jobs, why women don't get jobs, and it can determine the type of productions a woman is allowed to make. I often have to cut through layers of discrimination in the workplace, simply to be able to do my job – and that's not even factoring in my struggle with internalised misogyny in the form of undermining thoughts. Nowadays I don't mind being asked about my gender, and to be honest I think it would help enormously if male directors were asked, 'What is it like to be a male director?' This would allow a frank discussion about questions of maleness in terms of the work men make and the way they make it. Or you could ask men the question differently. You could ask, 'What does it feel like to read *Hamlet* as a man and to notice there is a wider spectrum of male experience and agency reflected back at you? And can you imagine what it feels like for me, a woman, to read *Hamlet* and to look at Gertrude and Ophelia and to see the pretty catastrophic internalised misogyny and mental health collapses going on?' Questions like this would, hopefully, encourage the male hegemony to realise that their version of things is simply that: one *version* of things. And that being male is about belonging to one of many identity groups in society. It doesn't mean your truth is the Absolute Truth or your outlook is the only outlook. Men urgently need to reposition themselves, and only when they start to talk about their gender and the oppression it can bring (both to themselves and others) can all the other identity groups in our society be offered the space they deserve. And, of course, you can't talk about gender or feminism without talking about how it intersects with issues like white supremacy. So, I don't think you need be nervous about asking women theatre-makers questions about their gender if you balance it by an equivalent interrogation of maleness. I choose to call myself a feminist theatre director because I am proud of being a woman and because all my work revolves around female experience. By describing myself like that I am saying that I stand up for equality and I'm prepared to take on the patriarchy and whatever it wants to throw at me. I also feel I have a duty of care to other women, particularly younger women at earlier points in their career. I want to model that talking about feminism is a positive and necessary thing.

Rebecca Frecknall

The poetic gesture of physicality, composition, movement and dance

Rebecca Frecknall is a multi-Olivier Award-winning theatre director working in the UK and internationally. She rose to prominence with her now-iconic 2018 revival of Tennessee Williams' *Summer and Smoke*, which transferred to the West End from the Almeida Theatre, where she is Associate Director. Following this, her work has included the multi-award-winning *Cabaret* at the Playhouse Theatre, starring Eddie Redmayne and Jessie Buckley in the original cast, and another five-star Tennessee Williams revival, this time of *A Streetcar Named Desire*, which opened at the Almeida in 2022 before transferring to the West End.

'The point of movement work is that it triggers you emotionally.'

Before training and working as a director, you did a lot of dancing. Could you start by giving an overview of your route into directing and, in particular, the transition from dance to theatre?

I always wanted to work in theatre, really. When I was a kid, I was obsessed with musical theatre – that's what I thought 'theatre' was, and what I wanted to do. It was also one of the reasons I did a lot of dancing. I had danced since I was around three years old and that was linked to liking musical theatre. But the more I danced, the more interested I became in it, and there was a point where I seriously considered going to study contemporary dance which, in retrospect, would not have been the right choice for me.

When I finished school, I had this very strong conviction that I didn't want to go to university. I wasn't interested in studying and I wanted to do theatre instead; at that point I actually wanted to go to drama school. But I ended up having two years out between finishing school and eventually going to university, and during that period of time I was dancing a lot, which is what made me think that maybe doing contemporary dance was the right path.

But, for one thing, I was never going to be good enough to do it professionally. You have to have such a specific body type. I was never naturally flexible and although I was a good dancer, I wasn't a great dancer, and to do the kind of work I wanted to do, I was never going to get to that level.

It was during these two sort of gap years that some actors, who I'm still in touch with, came to my dance studios to teach a Shakespeare evening class. It was pretty amazing because there were only three of us in the class and two teachers and, because the other students were still at school and doing their A levels, sometimes it would just be me and these two actors studying Shakespeare together. It was one of the best times I ever had; I just lived for those Tuesday nights. At that point I realised I wanted to do theatre – and thought that meant being an actor. But both of my teachers were like, 'Please don't be an actor! We don't think you're going to enjoy it!' They thought I should go to university and – eventually – I listened to them and ended up going to Goldsmiths to study Drama and Theatre Arts.

Initially I hated it! I was convinced I was right that I should never have gone to uni. But once I started to get into it, to understand the course and let my ego calm down a bit, I had such a great time, and it was then that I started directing. There was no drama society or extracurricular world at that point at Goldsmiths, but I was in a year group with Amy Letman, who went on to run Transform Festival in Leeds. She set up a new-writing festival because she also felt the lack of extracurricular activities for the theatre students. I really wanted to be involved but realised I couldn't just act in something when nothing had been made yet. So instead I wrote and directed a short play, and my friends performed it. It was the first thing I directed and I loved it. I suddenly went, 'Oh, this is everything I've wanted to do – I just didn't realise!'

From that point on, I knew I was going to be a director. So, after specialising in directing and devising in my second and third years, I graduated and went on to the directors' course at LAMDA. Since directing that first show, I never performed again and never wanted to. Directing just made complete sense to me, it was everything that stimulated me. I slogged away for ten years and kept trying – and failing. But eventually was given a shot.

And was that also the point where you felt like you'd left dance behind?

Not entirely. What I realised is that a lot of my dance training and interests came out in my work. For example, that first piece that I wrote and directed was quite a physical piece, and a lot of the elements were choreographed. It hasn't been a conscious decision but the more work I've made, the more it naturally emerged in that form. The physical language of what I make is very important to me, it's how I see the work and how I create it. I also had quite a physical introduction to theatre. The course at Goldsmiths was very postmodern, practical and experimental. It wasn't somewhere you studied plays in a cerebral, academic way. And if you made work, it was original work, not an existing text. I did a lot of dance-theatre work while I was there. In fact, I didn't actually direct an existing play until my final showcase at LAMDA when I, funnily enough, directed *Summer and Smoke* by Tennessee Williams. When I got to LAMDA, I was aware I was the least experienced director, in a conventional or classical way, on the course. And when I did work on plays, it was always quite an ensemble-based and physical-based production, because that's just how my work comes out.

I think my reference points and interests play a part, and my general artistic taste. But it's also because I find physicality and composition such an interesting mode of expression. A lot of my inspiration still comes from watching dance. More so than watching theatre, actually. It captures my inspiration in a different way. I'd never describe myself as a choreographer, but I can make movement, work with an actor's physicality and work with the composition of bodies in space. And craft the musicality of the work, as well. To me, it's an integral part of theatre. I don't think it is to everyone, but it always has been to me.

Nowadays, when you're working with actors on a new show, how does this interest in physicality manifest itself on a practical level? For example, do you have certain practices or exercises that you do in the rehearsal space to unlock that physical vocabulary?

It depends on the show. I never work with a movement director, I do that work myself, and what I've found is that I don't have one process I stick to every time. Instead, I have a toolbox of things that I often come back to, or that often crop up within a process but not necessarily in the same order or with the same focus. Some shows demand that the whole company has a shared physical language, whereas others require a focus on specific moments or specific characters.

For example, when I did *The Duchess of Malfi* at the Almeida in 2019, I knew that piece was going to require a shared physical language from everyone. And there was one specific thing I was interested in, which was working with what looks like slow motion – but is not 'slow motion'. It actually comes from the Michael Chekhov Technique, which I work with quite a lot. I've found it's an excellent type of physical work to do with actors because it's simple and universal. Actors also enjoy it because it 'doesn't feel like movement'. There are four different movement qualities within the Chekhov Technique – flying, floating, moulding and radiating – and they all generate different emotional triggers within the actor. Moulding is the one that looks like slow motion, which is what I wanted to use in *The Duchess of Malfi* because I was interested in playing with time, slowing it down and stretching it out and having two things happen at once. So with that show, I taught the company the four qualities in the first week of rehearsals. We went through the qualities, experimented with them, experienced them, and talked about the different emotional triggers they brought about in the actors. Because, really, the point of movement work is that it triggers you emotionally. This allows you to create genuine emotional and chemical changes in the room without being in danger of the work becoming too personally raw for the company.

When we got to the final quality, moulding, I explained to the actors that this was the quality we would be using in the physical language of the production, so we spent more time focusing on that one. That was great because once you've set up this shared language, everyone knows the references, and when you're working on things later you can say, 'With that sequence, could you do it again, but could you mould it?' and everyone is able to understand and experiment.

Then with *Summer and Smoke* in 2018, I used these movement qualities individually with Patsy Ferran, who was playing the protagonist Alma, because she had to be in a constant state of tension, and that can be quite a dangerous thing to do, physically, for eight shows a week. And to flip in and out of panic attacks. That play also included passages of dance in it, as did *Three Sisters*, which I worked on in 2019 [also at the Almeida]. In *Summer and Smoke*, Rosa dances for John, and in *Three Sisters*, all the young people dance together. I knew these moments were going to be much more choreographed, but I tended to keep the rehearsing of these moments as part of the general rehearsing of the scene. In my experience, actors can find it intimidating or get self-conscious if you're like, 'And now, the dance rehearsal!', so I tend to keep all the parts together, so you end up working on the dance part almost without noticing the shift from the scene work. I remember Ria Zmitrowicz, who played Irina in *Three Sisters*, described it as ninja choreography. She was like, 'You're tricking me into dancing without me realising!' And that's great, because it reduces the anxiety of having to learn steps and ensures the actors can easily remember the choreography, because it naturally evolved from their work in rehearsal and their own bodies.

Sometimes you have a company who find physically training together every day a particularly bonding experience and sometimes you have a group who prefer to do other things, like work more around the table. My general rule is that I like to split things up a bit and mix up activities. Personally, I don't like to sit down too long because I get itchy feet.

One thing I personally found interesting about *Summer and Smoke* was the visual composition – it was almost like the exact opposite of a classical, formal staging where everyone on stage is standing in straight lines, facing the audience. Are you consciously trying to do something quite formally radical in terms of how you place people on stage?

I'm not trying to be radical for the sake of it; I never make decisions solely for the sake of an aesthetic. I think, for me, it's about naturalism or realism – whatever we prefer to call it these days! – and how that connects to more poetic gestures. I like naturalism as an acting quality but as a visual quality it has never excited me. I admire it and I can be moved by it, but it's not something I've wanted to explore in the work I make. I've always been more interested in a poetic gesture on stage visually, and how you can marry a truthful – so in a way naturalistic but truthful – acting quality with a visual world that is poetic.

Summer and Smoke would be a good example because, in that play, the actors were aware of the reality of their characters, for example: 'I am in the drawing room of the vicarage.' But they were also working with the fact that they're on a wooden platform in a semicircle of pianos. I like working with a reduced palette because then you have these specific elements to work with, and the actors end up creating such interesting offers and pictures because it's impossible to come up with anything strictly naturalistic in that kind of a theatrical space.

What I love is trying to work out what the strongest elements of the set design are. Sometimes that involves working with a model box or coming up with an idea entirely in your head, and sometimes you look at the set and think, 'That will be the strongest place on the stage; that will make a great picture.' And then you get into the space with the actors and you're completely wrong! I like playing with the idea that a space accepts or rejects offers from the director and the actors, that the design is alive and is active as part of the rehearsal process.

For example, an actor might perform something and the space rejects it: it feels awkward or weak, or doesn't have the punch you thought it was going to have when you imagined it or saw it in the model box. But equally, the opposite can happen: someone places themselves somewhere you thought would be weak or odd and suddenly the whole thing comes together, the space accepts it and runs with it. So many of my favourite pictures or moments of visual composition in *Summer and Smoke* happened because the actors just found those positions and physical moments.

I do play games where you meet the set. Simple things, like I'll stand where the audience will be and the actors will all enter the space one by one and place themselves somewhere within it. It's such a simple practice, but you need to really, really do it and to really, really look and notice how the space and atmosphere shifts, notice what's strong and what's weak and when the picture dies, or you get bored. I find that very helpful. And then what happens is the actors solve a lot of the staging problems for you across the rehearsal process because they've worked out how to be playful with the design from the beginning.

Sometimes I will go, 'I want you there for that particular moment, because that looks great.' But I'll sometimes also stage things three or four different ways. Usually there is one way that is the strongest but if there isn't – and sometimes I've worked on shows where a scene can be done three different ways and I like them all equally – we will light that scene so it can be done three different ways and the actors can go down different paths with it. We did that quite a bit in *Three Sisters*.

For me, stage pictures can be so arresting and evocative. I knew, going into *Summer and Smoke*, that I wanted the first image to be this tiny woman at this microphone in a pool of light in the middle of nowhere, having a panic attack. I was very clear that was how I wanted it to start, and that never really shifted. I often, however, go into rehearsal with ideas of how things might go, and 90% of the time that's not the way we end up doing it. But despite that, I think it's important to arrive with a sense of what the first and last images of a play are going to be. It doesn't mean they have to come out like that but I like having a sense of how you're hooking your audience at both ends. The first image of a staging is very important, it's the first tool you have to get your audience on board. Most of the time, I don't know how the rest of the work will go but at least I'm playing between two points of clarity.

Along with an emphasis on movement and physical expression, do you think there is an overarching theme, concept or question that you keep returning to in your work as a whole?

Yes, I think there is. And I think it's sometimes been more subconscious than conscious. Something I learnt from Natalie Abrahami – who I worked with as an assistant director when I was first starting out – is that, as directors, we have to talk about our work quite a lot. And when you're starting out you have to have answers for questions like: 'What kind of work do you want to make?' or: 'What kind of work do you make?'

And you need to have this weird sort of tagline ready so people can understand or categorise you and your work. I hated that and was especially bad at doing it. And I remember talking to Natalie about it and she said that a good exercise is to look back at the work that you've done – not everything you've ever done, but the pieces that you feel represent you best as an artist – put them side by side and identify the themes of the plays, and the themes you've brought out of them, and that will tell you what you're actually working on.

Having done that, I discovered that the productions I have made and the plays I am drawn to all, pretty much, have female protagonists. That wasn't a deliberate conscious choice, but it obviously was on some subconscious level. But, in a way, that's just a recurring element. The themes that reappear and the themes I'm interested in exploring are loneliness, love, broken relationships, and the constant complexity around the need for human connection – or the impossibility of human connection.

Perhaps at the core of these themes are the questions: What is intimacy? Why do we crave and fear it? All the pieces I've done have been about that, in a way. I'm sure lots of artists and artworks are interested in that, but the plays I've worked on have all been about broken people with a huge hunger for intimacy. *A Streetcar Named Desire, Cabaret, Romeo and Juliet, Summer and Smoke, The Duchess of Malfi, Three Sisters* and *Miss Julie* – which I directed in 2016 at Northern Stage – were all about, to varying degrees, human intimacy, vulnerability and strength, faith and grief. It was interesting for me to explore, across all those plays, how these young women are trying, in their own ways, to survive and meet their needs within very complex societies.

I'm also interested in the flipsides of people. With all the plays I've named, we get to see the lead characters at their best and at their worst. I love that, it's so interesting to me. For example, Alma in *Summer and Smoke* can be so annoying! And she does awful things. She's narrow-minded and judgemental – but she's also strong, she loves, she's complicated and she has belief, real faith, which is rare. It's a joy working with an actor to excavate the extremes, nuances and contradictions of their character. That's the best bit, really. That's where the magic begins.

Yaël Farber

The body as a brain and the rite of theatre

Yaël Farber is a multi-award-winning South African playwright and director, whose work has been staged across the globe. Her career has spanned testimonial theatre, radical adaptations of Greek tragedies, earthy reimaginings of modern classics, and Shakespeare. Renowned for creating intensely atmospheric, sensory theatre, her work best known to UK audiences includes *Mies Julie* (premiered at the Edinburgh Festival Fringe in 2012), *The Crucible*, starring Richard Armitage, at The Old Vic (2014), and *Les Blancs* at the National Theatre (2016).

'You put a piece of yourself on the altar each night.'

Watching your work, I've constantly been struck by its very visceral, sensorial aspects and how the actors use their whole bodies to perform in a way that, I think, is very different to 'British' theatre – whatever someone takes that to mean. So, let's talk about bodies. Where does that word take you?

[*Laughs*] Oh god, lots to say about that! My rehearsal process is one wherein I try to make the actors initially aware of the degree to which our bodies are colonised by a socialisation that is committed to disconnecting us from our intuitions. I don't directly or politically talk about that, but I work through exercises to engage with the same concept. Sometimes I *will* use more direct language and pose questions like, 'How do we decolonise the body?' but more often I will suggest this more subliminally with provocations or physical directions. It depends who is in the room and what type of vocabulary will resonate with the given group. Directing is all about listening and reading the room, and knowing what works with different actors. But essentially, because I grew up in a country where, from a very young age, I was watching actors who engaged with so much more than this Cartesian idea of everything else being life support for the single 'thinking' part of the body, I've always understood the entire body to be a brain, in terms of deep intuitions and understandings. The body knows before the thoughts do. And so my process is committed to finding ways to release the actor from this kind of fascism of the brain that is so committed, as we often are culturally, to controlling the body. It centres on what it means to disinhibit. Because what you want is for people to be able to drop a thought process that is so embodied we almost mistake it for our personalities, or our preferences, whereas in fact it's culturally imposed. We need to ask, implicitly, what our relationship is to this: our body. And where should this body place itself in relation to other bodies?

So, I will often find ways of pushing the actors I am working with past that point of overthinking. For example, physical exertion takes you to a place of intuition. There are exercises that I've found and am always discovering in-process that can be very powerful ways of helping the actor unlock something. It might be that an actor is pressing into a wall for an extended period of time before returning to work with the text. The words they are saying have to come from the way the diaphragm engages, and the whole muscle of the body folds in around those gestures, pushing the words out into the world across the room to land on and affect the person standing opposite them. There's no part of your physicality that is left out of that.

I've never understood rehearsal rooms where directors create fear or ridicule to get actors to do what they want. I pursue ways to make people feel seen and held and understood in the process. Not in an indulgent way, but held with rigour in an environment where the rules are laid out very clearly and the limitations and parameters of the exercise are understood. Once you've created those boundaries, the possibilities are boundless.

When you say you've always understood, almost intuitively, the body to be one complex, interlinked, knowledgeable entity, did that come from the things you were watching in the theatre in South Africa, or was it a concept you were more explicitly taught?

No, I don't think I was taught it. When I was a child, I was watching theatre that was an aspirational imitation of British theatre in the white playhouses of Apartheid South Africa, with all its inherited vestigial understandings of how theatre was 'done'. Its message, along with its form, felt so disconnected and disconnecting to me. I've often told the story of being taken to see a musical as a child of about six or seven years old – it may or may not have been *Annie* – and coming out of this all-white theatre in the all-white suburbs to see the horizon filled with smoke. I was told the people of the township of Soweto were 'rioting' – which is a very particular choice of word. What was actually happening was the Soweto uprising by schoolchildren, which resulted in a massacre as police brutally suppressed the protests. I remember feeling this unnameable but vast disjuncture between us watching this very vanilla musical, while on the horizon – it looked like war – children were dying not ten kilometres away. As a young teenager, some years later, I discovered the Market Theatre in Johannesburg. Because of a loophole in the law connected to marketplaces, this was a theatre where actors of all races could perform together and audiences of all races could sit alongside each other. I discovered there that the artists of this kind of theatre were pushing past the lies that we had been told and through the shimmer that had been created to prevent people like myself from understanding what was actually happening in the country. Here was a theatre that was not the opiate or distraction of the people, but the awakening of its intended audience. What struck me full force were the full-flung bodies in that room: singing, moving, grabbing, striking, coming into the faces of the audience, pouring with sweat… and a light went on; it was a circuit connector for me. It wasn't just about being told the truth, it was believing the instruments that were telling me the truth via the headlong hurl of the body into that message and into that communication. I understand the absolute magnificence of restraint. But there has to be so much moving underneath it. A lot of the theatre I watch is neck-up. It's fiercely clever, but the body is kind of dead and disengaged from below. When the lights are not on and the eyes of the body are closed, I can't feel what I'm watching. And I think we feel theatre more than we hear it or see it. Of course, all those faculties are there. But ultimately, I just know whether I'm feeling what I'm watching or not.

Let's move on to talking then about how you work with actors to perform in a way that isn't 'dead from the neck down'. How easy is it for actors – particularly those who have been trained in, shall we say, a very different tradition – to unlock that way of working with their bodies?

It can be very difficult for some people. And I have worked with actors who just don't want to go on that journey – I and they thought they would be up for it, but they weren't, maybe because our idea of ourselves is often different from the reality – and I've worked with others who quickly unlock something magnificent. The audition process tells you a lot. Not so much about capability but willingness. Every body, even if it's awkward committing to that form and way, has its beauty, because it's true. It can be very exciting to watch how people work within the constraints of the country of their body to push beyond its borders – if they are willing to do so. Interestingly, I sometimes find that people who consider themselves to be physical performers can be less interesting than actors who don't think of themselves as that at all.

Why so?

In everything we do, the greatest adversary I'm working to overcome in the room with the actor is self-regard. By which I mean, the act of the actor witnessing themselves as they're doing what they do. There are actors who have refined their artillery – in terms of movement – to such an astonishing degree that it's an incredible language, so I'm not saying actors who are physically trained are not the ones I want. Because working with that type of actor is akin to directing Chekhov with people who speak fluent Russian: it's beautiful and has a vocabulary way beyond what I have. And those people can offer you so much when you make a request. You'll get seven choices back from them each time you pose a question. But what's interesting is often actors who are dance-trained, for example, will struggle a great deal to find a release outside the discipline they have been taught. I danced for many years and I acted for two or three years. And one reason I was never going to be the kind of actor that I would ever cast or direct was because my body had been taught a different neutral. Neutral for me was (in the flamenco tradition) a profoundly arched back. A dance-trained body already has all these layers built up that require a whole other process to crack off before a simple truth emerges. This is true too for an overly gymed body or any physicality over-identified with form already. There's a magnificent Peter Brook quote where he talks about how there are some actors who just simply cannot put down the way they consider themselves and become available to the work. And you may never access the raw openness the work may need from them. Others have an innate freedom or at least the willingness to plough into the work that it takes to transcend the corsets of our conditioning.

So, when I audition people, I'm looking for those who can or are curious to try. It's a humble pursuit. The beginner's mind. Once we get into the rehearsal room, we're pursuing the disinhibited state that allows something true to emerge. There's a lot of presuppositions of how an actor is supposed to stand on stage, for instance, and I find I'm often encouraging the artists to undo that work. When I am watching theatre, I acutely feel the artifice that arises from bodies being trapped in the ways they are presenting themselves to the audience. But I've also worked with film actors who have no idea how to open the generosity of the body to the room. They don't have the training. So training is golden. Curiosity to fly with it in new ways is what interests me.

But above all that – or alongside it – I'm trying to bring bodies back to recover them from the legacy of the Abrahamic religions. Whether we're religious or not, we're taught to behave towards our bodies in a way that once decided: 'We are not allies.' We believe we have to overcome things about our bodies that shouldn't be happening or which do happen, and it's some kind of test to overcome the temptations of those things. It's a cultural inheritance that goes back thousands of years. We cannot know what Greek tragedy genuinely looked like in the amphitheatres, but it would have to have been committed enough in every fibre of the body that ten thousand people could watch it without the technology we have today. And that is the spirit that I still chase.

Can you tell me some more about the kind of exercises you use to enable actors to work in this way, and how you run the rehearsal room?

I spend a lot of time making a safe room. Not through censoring or restricting what we do, but by saying to the actors, 'These are your mechanisms for when you need to step away: you raise your right hand and/or you press your back up against the wall if you are going beyond your own parameters of what is safe.' I can't know everyone's personal history, so I won't always know if something in an exercise is going to make someone feel triggered. But I can create a space in which you in no way feel pressured to continue in something that you are not comfortable with. And if you're not comfortable, you can signal that without other people feeling like they fucked up or did something wrong, or without totally breaking the spell of the room. It's my responsibility to set up the room in a way where everyone is sovereign unto themselves and is able to let me know if we're approaching their limits or unexpectedly hitting up against something uncomfortable beyond what they can offer.

I am in charge of the room, so everyone can be assured there is not weak leadership. Nor is there favouritism or bullying. I am very, very demanding, but I demand the most that one is able to give. And no one should ever feel shame if they aren't able to go where the rest of the group is going. I think, in this way, people feel empowered in the room. I love the 'creatureness' of guiding people into their bodies. In the room we talk a lot about why the work is important, which links to that Viktor Frankl equation of how people can tolerate anything as long as there's a purpose. We need purpose – the artists need to know and feel why we are making this work. If there is a culture that's focused on getting great reviews, well then, we're fucked. Because my work is never going to operate in those ways. The other thing I do is ask that people don't speak about the work beyond the room. That includes telling a fellow cast member on their lunch break that they were amazing in a given day's work. Because, as every director knows, if you tell an actor something is amazing, they are going to spend the rest of their time trying to get back to what was amazing, and it will never be amazing again. And don't spend your time away from the room talking about the work to your lover in bed, because they will invariably weigh in and then I've got seventy-five other directors to contend with. I want people to feel they can be foolish in the room, try things and mess up, and that not be spoken about in ways that make us want to play safe. I mean, everyone is an adult. They can ultimately do as they wish beyond the room, but it's hugely powerful when you have a company who can keep all the charge and power and trust in the room. I need people who are going to turn up and believe in the magic we're trying to make. For a couple of weeks, we're all going to build a little community and we're going to believe in the magic; we're going to believe that we are literally creating, for example, the blasted heath.

You mentioned the importance of creating a sense of safety in the room. Is that something you learnt from your own experiences of being an actor?

Definitely. I remember being in rooms that I didn't trust. I didn't trust the leadership. I didn't trust them for competence, let alone for safety. I wanted to be making something extraordinary and a lot of the time I didn't feel excited about being there. I didn't feel like we were in the business of uncompromisingly searching for the truth. And that's the place I always want to be in. We're all here, probably being underpaid, but we're here because – hopefully – we still believe in the reasons for which we first decided we wanted to be part of storytelling. I wanted that currency to be alive in the room when I was an actor, and I want it to be there now I am a director. It sounds patronising, but it's like with good parenting where you say, 'I want you to reach your full potential and these are the parameters.' You've got to consider others and be aware that you might overstep their limits without knowing it, which is why I have that gesture I described to allow people to signal when they have had enough. If you make people go way beyond what is intuitively manageable for them, then the work we are making won't be sustainable. But I need to find a way for people to connect with their intuitions and their bodies. We want to row the boat out beyond the breakers.

There's a very deep gendering to how the intuitive aspects of ourselves have been delegitimised. Over the past thousand or so years, the collective has tended towards the individual; the agrarian has tended towards the industrial, and the body and its intuitions can no longer be trusted. Even the cycles of the seasons can no longer be trusted. And I think that shows up very much in our losses inside our experience of theatre. We've turned it into such a particular exercise.

And that being a capitalist endeavour. The celebrity names, the essential mandate of the five-star reviews. To return again to Peter Brook, he articulates it perfectly: 'Over the centuries the Orphic Rites turned into the Gala Performance – slowly and imperceptibly the wine was adulterated drop by drop.' When you think of the image of these ancient amphitheatres where the city came to consider themselves and to really be taken through their paces; where men returning from war to the domestic space would watch *Oedipus Rex* or *Medea* as a part of reintegrating themselves with dependent living – and the complete disconnect between that ideal and the capitalist contemporary pursuit of selling theatre – we are at odds with its origins.

When I directed *Hamlet* with Ruth Negga in Dublin, a friend came to see it and afterwards he texted me: 'Now that was a rite not a right.' Hamlet is a role containing the possibility to embody the very nature of all the considerations of our existence. Its achievement is staggering as a work. It's a role that, if it doesn't cost you almost everything, you're not doing it properly. But we've turned it into this thing where people feel they have a right to ask, 'When do I get to do my Hamlet?' Because they've gone through certain motions and jumped through certain hoops. It stops being this unbelievably upending, exhausting, demanding rite in which you sacrifice yourself for the audience. I know this language might be off-putting to some. I use it because I am someone who tends towards the holy theatre, and away from the domestic and the prosaic. The theatre that I saw as a teenager coming of age was a place of truth at all costs in a fascist context that wanted all forms of expression to corroborate their lies. And I have never fallen out of love with that pursuit. With a truly sacrificial theatre, you put a piece of yourself on the altar each night and then, and only then, is the full velocity of the magic possible.

Nancy Medina

Getting out of the head and into the body

In March 2023, Nancy Medina became the Artistic Director of Bristol Old Vic. Alongside being a founding co-Artistic Director at the Bristol School of Acting until 2022, she has directed work at venues including Kiln Theatre, Bush Theatre and Young Vic. She was the winner of the Genesis Future Directors Award, the RTST Sir Peter Hall Director Award, the NT Peter Hall Bursary, and in 2023 she was shortlisted for the Genesis Foundation Prize 2024. Her critically acclaimed production of *Trouble in Mind* played the National Theatre in 2021, while her other work includes *Choir Boy* at Bristol Old Vic (2023), *The Darkest Part of the Night* at Kiln Theatre (2022), *Strange Fruit* at the Bush Theatre (2019) and *The Half God of Rainfall* for Fuel, Kiln Theatre and Birmingham Rep (2019).

'Theatre gives us that little bit of space to be present, to be human...'

Prior to becoming the Artistic Director at the Bristol Old Vic, you were a co-Artistic Director and founder of the Bristol School of Acting. Before talking about your expertise as a director, I wanted to start by talking a little about your extensive experience teaching actors at the BSA and elsewhere, and how that links up with your work in the rehearsal room and on stage. But first, what was the original idea behind setting up the school?

I first started working with Stuart Wood, the BSA's Head of School and my co-AD, when he invited me to help him establish an acting course for young people which would, in essence, give them a head start in their pre-drama-school training by offering them an introduction to a kind of conservatoire-style of training. I had done a lot of teaching in my hometown of New York and I thought: why not? I began by teaching the students the Meisner technique, which is what I was taught when I was younger and training to be an actor, and also an approach I've used a lot as a director. That in itself was interesting because of how Meisner teaching has developed over the last few years and the ways in which you need to adapt it for younger people. With Meisner, the focus is on repetition, listening and observing physical behaviour. As much as I am a text person, I do believe the audience get so much of the story through the physical language and behaviour on stage. The nuanced ways we communicate non-verbally. The story is actually being told through the offers actors make to each other – what they pick up and what they let go. Anyway, after several years working with sixteen- to nineteen-year-olds in this way, Stuart said, 'Hey, I'm thinking of doing BA courses, would you like to run the school with me?!' By this point I was very busy with my own directing, but it's the highlight of my year working with students. It's hard and has been especially hard over the past few years with the pandemic as it has involved a lot of pastoral care in response to mental health issues. But with young people, anything is possible. When you see that inspiration and flash of light, when you see them believing in themselves, it's like nothing else – and I love that. So I said, 'Yes, let's do this!' But I also said that, if we were going to do it, we needed to do it differently. We'd both worked in drama schools and understood that institutions can get stuck in their ways. It felt like we had all become fixated on training products for the industry and we wanted to break away from that.

Our question became: 'How do you create a drama-training programme with the actor as artist?' Our understanding was that all acting students bring with them qualities that are interesting, special and inspiring, and if they become theatre-makers in their own right as well as actors then the industry will start to change. We also appreciated the importance of training actors to a certain level so they could get jobs. The technique had to be good and their abilities had to enable them to graduate and succeed in an industry where it's getting harder and harder for actors to secure jobs. But we also wanted to empower students to be able to have real critical conversations with directors and producers, so they were more than just a pawn in a big old game. This might include, for example, having a discussion about colour-blind versus colour-conscious casting, and what it means to bring your lived experience to a classic (default white) role. For me, the most exciting thing about starting the school was being able to have the conversations with young people that they previously felt too afraid or too powerless to have. They should be able to have these conversations because that's going to make better theatre in the future.

Do you think that students who graduate from the BSA are an integrally different kind of actor to those who have trained elsewhere?

I hope so. I heard something depressing a few years ago. Someone had said to me, 'I can watch a show and I can totally see that, oh, that's so-and-so school…' And I thought, 'Wow, that's not good.' If you can see an actor's training like that it means you're not seeing the individual actor with their own talents and what they can truly bring to a work. I hope the BSA graduates are completely individual so that you won't be able to tell where they've been trained. That's actually where their training starts. The whole first term is about a self-story, about finding out about themselves, which is scary, exposing and vulnerable. But it's also what makes the actors I worked with there so confident in the end, because they don't have to hide who they are. It meant they understood what their weaknesses and strengths were, and what they needed to develop, rather than depending on us as tutors or directors telling them where they needed to go. By working alongside us – the teaching staff – it also made the set-up feel less hierarchical.

Is an actor's training background something you're aware of in the rehearsal space? In particular, do you ever feel that actors turn up to work with you and they're carrying baggage from their own training that you have to help them put down?

Yes and no. Unlike a lot of American directors who have a clear philosophy of acting, I am more of a magpie. I want to understand lots of different techniques and help the actor work in the way they find most effective. For example, I can discern if an actor takes more of a logistic or analytical approach and know how to support that. A few years ago, I was struggling with this actor because it felt like we weren't able to communicate. That was until one day when I realised they were used to working with actions and actioning. It's not an approach I usually use but, from my teaching, I understand it and I was able to use it with him. He was an older actor who was coming back to the theatre after a long gap, and it was so important that I was able to understand his process so we could work well together. As a director, it's really important to just be a good listener because that's how you'll help the actors to communicate on stage.

Also, it's worth saying that technique and training are great, but they only get you so far. As an actor, you can learn an accent or choreography. But the most important work is being able to look at the world through the lens of the character, which involves an individual genuinely looking at their own framework of thinking, and then adopting the different framework of thinking of a character. For example, you can be trained to perform a character that has a speech impediment, but if you don't understand how that character goes through their daily life – how they buy their groceries, how they're perceived and how they perceive themselves – then you can't really delve into that character fully. The most precious thing about acting is understanding the lens through which their character views the world. And when that's different to yours then that's even more exciting! Because then you've got lots of things to discover.

Returning to your comment about working with students to uncover stories and be quite vulnerable, does that ever result in students unlocking personal stuff that is then difficult to deal with?

When I was at the BSA, we started working with a drama therapist, so we had some protection around that. The last few years have been a particularly hard time for young people and it's difficult, in general, to know when someone's going to find something overwhelming, so we took as many precautions as we could. With the drama therapist, the work all started with looking at how you create rituals to protect yourself when you're working on vulnerable material, because it's a fact that, as professional actors, they are going to have to. They need to acquire an understanding of how you start something, work on it, and then you find a way of ending it and leaving it in that room. And those kinds of rituals manifest themselves in different ways, but it's so important to understand that it's work that you're doing. It's hard for all theatre artists, not just actors, because what we do is so much 'us'. And sometimes that's hard to separate. For a long time, I found it difficult to separate myself from my work, especially the stories I tell because there's a lot that connects to my childhood and things I'm still figuring out. But I have found a way to say, 'That is the work and I am me' – and that separation is important for a healthy life.

Do you have your own rituals for doing that?

I have really good boundaries at the moment. When I know that I'm going to be working on hard material, I have a space and time where I'm going to be delving into that hard material, and then I let it go. If it's on the computer or I'm writing down my thoughts in my journal, I see that as working at the computer or writing in my journal, and then I put an end to it and I do the next thing. For example: now it's time with my family, that stuff is done, and I don't continue thinking about it. I also try very hard not to talk to my husband about my work either. There's something very useful about separating it so that I have the framework: this is work, it's not me. It's not doing my own therapy, it's work. My rituals change and evolve but right now they're about having fixed times for when I'm doing the work, and for when I'm being 'me'.

You mentioned how much you got from working with young people as a teacher. In terms of your own identity, do you see 'Nancy the teacher' as being separate from 'Nancy the director' and, most recently, 'Nancy the artistic director'? Are these separate entities or are they all kind of meshed together?

I do see them separately because I'm different in each of them. Whatever I'm doing, I care about everybody I work with, and I try to create very safe rooms. But with teaching, that's particularly the case because the people I'm teaching are young and therefore vulnerable and, often, come from marginalised communities – for example, I've worked with lots of young carers. There's a sensitivity that I always bring to that work. Which isn't to say I'm not sensitive with professionals but that you can push professionals and grown-ups in ways you shouldn't with younger students. You can also talk about more abstract ideas with grown-ups whereas I think with students you need to guide them through things and answer a lot more questions to help them get to where they need to go. And as far as 'Nancy the artistic director' is concerned… well, I've just got the job so I'm still figuring that out!

Let's return to the comment you made earlier about audiences getting so much of the story through physical language and behaviour on stage. How do you enable actors to access a place where they're acting, in a sense, through their bodies rather than simply delivering lines?

I take scripts away pretty quickly! Normally, I will start a rehearsal period with only two days at the table reading the script, understanding what's happening, identifying major themes, and having conversations, and then I do a process of feeding in. This means the actors are up on their feet, without scripts, and someone is feeding in the lines. The feeder needs to do this in a monotone way, without giving any inflections. If an actor hasn't heard something, or they need it to be slower, all they have to do is ask and the line gets repeated again. But without having the script in hand, they're just observing their partner. They have no idea what the next line is and when it is coming, so it feels much more spontaneous. What I've heard from a lot of actors I've worked with in this way is that they end up learning their lines better. Thanks to the repetition and having to do it on your feet, there's a muscle memory attached to it. Not every actor loves feeding in, and you have to be okay with that. Some actors love having their scripts, which is fine because everybody's a different type of learner and sometimes people need the visual and the 'feel' of the script.

I started using this method because when I was an actor I would learn my monologues with a feeding-in process, and because there's something about allowing the words to drop through this process. You sort of allow them to drop into your tummy by dropping the breath and seeing how different words hit you. Unexpectedly, I've also found that a high number of actors are dyslexic and have difficulties with a script, which makes feeding in much better for them. It's also beneficial on so many levels because you're getting people up on their feet and, very quickly, they're moving without thinking about how they're moving. They're concentrating on the other characters or what's happening in the space. There's a certain relaxation that happens, because you know your lines are going to come from somewhere. It's very freeing.

Are there other things that you took from your own experiences of being an actor that you now use in the rehearsal space?

Again – Meisner training! I never officially trained, instead I did lots of part-time classes. But I remember when I first discovered actioning, I thought it was amazing. Ordinarily, if you want to, say, seduce or act angrily, you're in control to do so. But Meisner takes away that control and makes it all about your partner, not about you. That was so freeing for me, because it took me out of my head and helped me to be in my body. It also helped me to be in my emotions and respond intuitively. I've really taken that into my work as I always encourage actors to get out of their heads. There's an intellectual understanding that we all have about what we're doing, but what we're responding to on stage are the things society doesn't allow us to do. We don't allow ourselves to expand these moments of being real humans in regular society, because we've got jobs, we've got rent to pay, we've got all the stresses of life. But theatre gives us that little bit of space to be present, to be human, to take time to address the emotions we ride over as normal human people during the day. I think that's so important. And I definitely think that that's what I took from acting into my directing.

Going back to when you're working with actors in the rehearsal room, how would you go about resolving conflict – for example, somebody's not quite gelling with somebody else or something's not quite working, and an actor is struggling to get in touch with what's happening and what you're doing?

That's a really difficult one. In my last four or five professional shows, I've had a drama therapist on hand because my work tends to delve into hard topics that will sometimes bring up trauma for people because they have lived experience of the same thing. It's much safer to have a drama therapist to support that. But as far as actors who are disagreeing with each other or maybe not liking each other goes, yeah, I've completely had that over the years! It's very rare but I've had a couple of instances of it and with both it was a case of taking each person aside, understanding what the issue was, and asking how I could help. We need to make the room as professional as possible, but also understand there are some obstacles in the way. In one instance, I had to have a mediation with both the actors to help them understand what the issue was with each other, and how we could move on professionally to continue the work. Remember we are all human and that comes first. No one has to be best friends in these situations. It's wonderful when a cast fall in love with each other and become great friends. But professionally speaking, actors also understand that it's a job and when something starts hindering the art you're making, you have to step in, remind people why they are there and not let these things go too far. It's not easy! The two situations I was just thinking about were so hard.

Do you have a mechanism in your rehearsal room whereby actors can voice concerns they may have? How would they do that and who would they go to?

A few years ago, especially after one horrendous experience making a production where there were quite a lot of mental health issues, I created a rehearsal process which begins, on day one, with talking about a mental health toolkit. The question is: 'If there were three things in your mental health toolkit, what would they be? Would you want a break-out space? Would you want to set up a signal with me for when you need to leave the room? Would you want to say, actually, with a hard scene, I only want to do it once and not over and over again?' Just things like that – and it could be anything. People don't have to share their answers with the group, they can come to me privately and let me know. I've found that break-out spaces are particularly popular, but there's been some interesting other stuff as well. In one rehearsal room, an actor asked to have their drawing pad present. Then, on breaks, they would doodle and do some drawing. That was great, because the rest of the cast then did it as well – it became the art corner! I've found that by asking about mental health toolkits on day one of the read-through, far fewer things come up throughout the rehearsal period because people feel more secure. In fact, about half the time when people have told me what they need in their toolkit, they haven't even needed it, because they know it's there if they need it. It's when you don't put these things in place that things can go awry.

You said you're still figuring out what Nancy the artistic director is going to be like, but tell me a bit about your general ambitions and vision for being that person. What does a Bristol Old Vic with you at the helm look like?

Bristol is my hometown. I've lived here for fifteen years and when the position came up I was encouraged by a few people to apply. Bristol is a very young city, and a city of innovation and protest and rebellion. But it's also very complicated and segregated city. Indeed, the very infrastructure of our city breaks different neighbourhoods apart, meaning there are pockets of Bristol that feel so different to other pockets of Bristol. There are lots of cultural groups that never get any attention whatsoever. I want us to tap into that spirit of rebellion and creativity, but I also want us to be having some hard conversations about who we are and who we are making theatre for. One of the things I said early on was that I never want to hear, '…because that's the way it's always been done.' I never want to hear that. I want to hear, 'This is a problem and let's figure out how we can beat this problem.' We need to be thinking about what our civic duty is as a cultural institution and which of our audiences have been missing out for a long time. Changes aren't going to happen overnight, but we need to be working toward something.

Then in terms of programming as an artistic director, I don't think that is a question of personal taste. It's about understanding who your audience is. The essential questions are: Why do we gather these people together? Why do people gather? Why do people need to see this story? Why do they need to see this story now? And in what form does this story need to be? As a freelance theatre director, I've always had my audience in mind and they're normally a Black and brown audience – that's who I'm speaking to. As a director I want all people to come and see my work, but the stories I want to tell are for those particular people. But bringing this back to my new role as artistic director of an organisation, I definitely want to see more stories about people from the global majority and protected classes on our stages, as part of a balanced programme of work that serves the whole community equally. I really would love my Bristol Old Vic to be a place of innovation, where people come to try out ideas and new stories, and we give them a home.

Marianne Elliott

Shutting out comparisons and having space to fail

Marianne Elliott is the Artistic Director of Elliott & Harper Productions, the company she founded with Chris Harper and Nick Sidi. As a multi-award-winning director whose accolades include multiple Olivier and Tony awards, she has made work for venues across the West End and Broadway, along with an extensive collection of shows for the National Theatre. Earlier in her career, she was an associate director at the Royal Court and was one of four Artistic Directors at the Manchester Royal Exchange. Her best-known work includes *War Horse* (2007), *The Curious Incident of the Dog in the Night-Time* (2012), *Angels in America* (2017), *Company* (2018) and *Death of a Salesman* (2019).

'You choose your family and you close the door.'

When I've interviewed younger female directors in recent years, one subject that repeatedly comes up is this idea of creating theatre for large-scale spaces and, in particular, being 'trusted' to make that leap. You're someone with a huge amount of experience making theatre for the biggest spaces available – the National, the West End, Broadway and so forth – so I wanted to open by asking you about precisely that. Firstly, does making work for a space like the National Theatre's Olivier auditorium mean you're faced with very specific considerations?

Yes, it does. It's very different. However, it's worth starting by saying that, when I was younger, I thought I preferred smaller spaces! Early on, I saw a lot of work at the Manchester Royal Exchange where no audience member is more than thirty feet away from the actors. What I love most about theatre is the skill of the actor, so I always wanted the audience to be as close to that as possible. Also, when I started making theatre at the Royal Exchange it was just after the [1996] Manchester bomb had collapsed the main theatre space – which normally seats about 750 – so instead we were making shows for this sort of makeshift tent which only seated about 230 people. I then made theatre for the Royal Court, where both theatres are, relatively speaking, small stages. It was only when I got to the National Theatre that I started making shows for much bigger spaces. I had created only one piece of work for the NT when the then-Artistic Director Nicholas Hytner asked me to become an associate, which was a huge shock. When I got over that shock, I told him I would love to be an associate, but I didn't want to work in the Olivier because I only wanted to work in small spaces. And he sort of just hummed. The next show to come up for me was the possibility of directing Bernard Shaw's *Saint Joan* in the Olivier. I read the play and I said, 'I love this, I can really see a way of doing it, but I don't feel very comfortable about the Olivier.' And Nick said, 'Oh, you'll be fine.' That was it, he literally just said, 'Oh, you'll be fine'!

So, I was possibly the opposite to a lot of people you've interviewed previously in that I never wanted to be in a big space. And I wasn't given a huge amount of support, other than the fact I *was* given a huge amount of support because I was literally pushed in there and told I'd be fine, which in a way was hugely supportive. Funnily enough, once I did *Saint Joan,* the Olivier became my favourite space of all the theatres at the National – and remains so today.

But to return to the question, yes, there are very, very different considerations when you're making work for that kind of theatre. What I love most is that you can make grand gestures and deliver large-scale visual messages. Inevitably, the budget is also larger – or it certainly used to be – and you're allowed more people in the cast. I do a lot of commercial work now and that always requires something pretty grand. Even when I directed Mike Bartlett's *Cock* in the West End, which had no set as such, no props, no changes of location and just four actors on stage, it required a kind of operatic mentality.

You described yourself then as being most interested in the skill of the actor. Do actors need to be doing something different when they're performing in really big spaces?

Yes – and also no, in some senses. I don't like relying on mics very much. Maybe I'm quite old-school, as far as that is concerned. But, for me, actors need to really work on their voices in order to hit the back wall and then sustain that through a long run. That's a muscle requirement and it's not just a technical thing, it's a mental thing as well. It's a mental shift that requires serious engagement; you have to work on your voice properly for quite some time before you hit the stage.

You can also get away with very large theatrical performances in a large space, which you wouldn't be able to in a smaller space. They can be quite performative or stylised, but you can also do performances that are very real. The most important thing with a large space is to work out the dynamics of it. Every space is different, and you need to figure out what the dynamics of the space are so the audience are engaged. With the Olivier, the dynamics are quite specific, especially if it isn't configured in the round. The main word I would use here is focus: you have to know how to absolutely focus the audience's attention. So you can do a tiny gesture, something really real – like more real than real – but you have to also know how to make the audience see it.

How do you do that? I mean, what are your – I don't want to say 'tricks', but – mechanisms for focusing an audience's attention on a certain gesture or aspect?

You have to take your audience by the hand. There are lots of conversations about not treating your audience as though they're stupid and, to a certain extent, I agree. But you also have to be gentle with them and lead them through a story. If you want to make a massive grand gesture, that's great, but be careful with where you're guiding people. It can all look like a big mess if you're not in control of what you want the audience to be looking at and receiving from what you're doing. Sometimes, as a director, it's an instinctive thing, whereas other times it takes me until I'm sitting in the auditorium in previews to be able to sense the audience aren't quite getting a moment. It's hard to put into words why you know they're not, because they're not moving and they're not saying anything and they're in exactly the same position as they were a couple of seconds ago, but it's just a feeling you get. Which, of course, is why theatre is so amazing, because you can get a feeling just from being in the room when nobody is moving or saying anything. It's ultimately about guiding. For example, 'This is a grand gesture moment; this is a moment where we all go wild. This is a big visual sequence, and now this is a tiny gesture you need to look at.'

You mentioned the mental shift actors need to make to be able to perform well in a larger space. Have you ever worked with actors who have found that shift difficult, and what did you do to help them?

I work with some brilliant voice coaches. They're integral to most of the things I've done, yet there aren't that many good ones left in the industry. Maybe it's a skill that's gone slightly out of fashion, I don't know. But they're absolutely key to helping actors get themselves to the right place. It's also to do with the actor's energy, stamina and living their life sort of like a nun! Or, as I often say, you have to treat the job as though you're a professional athlete. You can't do much else for the duration of the run; you have to dedicate all your energy to being onstage every day. You have to eat well, you have to sleep well. It's about getting your head in the right mental state and knowing what muscles you need to train to help the way you breathe and therefore speak. It's also about technical exercises. For example, this is a generalisation, but with many classic plays the point of the speaking line is at the end of the sentence. And we, as humans in 2023, tend to drop our voices and our stresses at the end of our sentences. But with a classic text the most powerful word is usually at the end, which means you need to retrain to break our colloquial habit. And doing things like that requires a huge amount of discipline and practice. Especially if it is to come across as natural and real.

Does creating work for large spaces come with a bigger set of risks and pressure than creating work for smaller spaces? I mean, is directing a show for the Olivier a bigger ask all round to making something for the Dorfman?

In my experience, yes. Even more so if you work in commercial theatre because commercial theatre is all about getting the audiences in so you can pay the investors back and recoup the show. And, if you're lucky, the producers also make a bit of money on top of that which helps to make the next show! If you're working for a subsidised theatre, that's slightly different. But in the end, you're only seen as being as good as your last show, which means you're constantly trying to be adventurous and do something different to prove yourself. This encourages risk – which is a good thing! In the commercial world, the pressure is greater because the number of people that come through the door means a lot. You're constantly considering: Have you got enough people buying tickets? Have you got a big enough star? Is it a show people want to see? How is it reviewed? Is it hitting the zeitgeist? Will it run as long as you want it to? Followed by: Will it get a transfer or an extension? The concerns are never-ending. Personally, you're still pushing for taking risks, and making something wonderfully creative. But you have to juggle the two – which can be tricky!

How do you, on a personal level, cope with that pressure? How do you stop all that from keeping you up at night?

Well, if only I knew the answer to that…! I think, somewhere inside me, there is a constant drive to do something exciting in theatre. And that means not boring and not easy. It means something that somebody has not done before. Every time I do a show, I think, 'Oh my God, why am I so ambitious? Why don't I just do "blah-blah"? Why am I doing this in this way? This is crazy.' But I was brought up in a theatrical family. Both sides, maternal and paternal, worked in theatre. So, I went to see a lot of theatre growing up, it was absolutely part of what we did – go to the theatre together, and at that time a lot of what was out there was quite conventional, perhaps boring theatre. Which left me with the complete conviction I might as well not bother contributing to any more of that. I'm really, really passionate about theatre as an art form, which drives me to take risks and to do more interesting things – whether they fail or succeed – and yet to try to get a big audience for it.

Speaking of your early ambition and drive, when you collected the Tony Award for *Company*, you remarked that, growing up, you hadn't imagined becoming a director because you thought all directors were men – and, at the time, they were. What has your experience of being a female director in the British theatre industry been like?

It's been varied, a mix of good and bad. I was lucky because when I was coming up the ranks, people were aware there weren't many female directors and they started to feel they had to do something about that. I capitalised on that, and I genuinely think I was given quite a few jobs because I was one of the few female directors who were coming up at the time. So I lucked out.

However, it's had its downsides as well. They're slightly more difficult to pinpoint because it's to do with attitudes, which are hard to call out. I remember one planning meeting at a theatre I was an associate at, where all the execs were there, and the top people, and someone said, 'Oh, Marianne, you just like those stories about women having a hard time.' And everybody laughed – and I laughed. But afterwards, I thought, 'But isn't that what *Hamlet* is? *Hamlet* is about a man having a hard time, isn't it? So what's your problem with that?' I mean, all drama is about something dramatic happening, which usually means a tension connected to wanting something that's difficult to get. So the protagonist is having a hard time. And, yes, I like female protagonists on the whole. So it did feel odd and uncomfortable to be the butt of that joke. I didn't quite understand it.

Also, when I was working on my very first show, I worked with an actor who was very difficult. I felt that was because I was a young female, and he wasn't listening to me. The fact is, sometimes there are issues over authority because, whether we like it or not, it's still very much a patriarchal society.

But there are so many things that are beneficial about being a woman. You have to excuse the huge generalisations, but if you're working with a bunch of people who are willing to be vulnerable in order to find the best way to tell a story and portray a character, then it can help them to be with somebody who is sympathetic, who makes them feel safe, who makes them feel included, who knows how to help, who isn't particularly interested in ego, who is much more interested in the group dynamic. All of those things, which are traditionally seen as female traits, can benefit the process.

Did that awareness of being given opportunities because people wanted to encourage more female directors come with an added

weight of responsibility? Did you ever feel you needed to succeed to prove women in general could, or anything like that?

I'm not sure. There was certainly pressure to prove myself on every show. At the Royal Exchange, everyone was a man apart from me. At the Royal Court, almost everyone was a man. And at the National, almost everyone was a man. And perhaps that did lead to feeling pressure, as a woman. But I also simply felt pressure because of the expectations I had of myself to be successful. In terms of comparisons to others, the pressure I felt most acutely was connected to not being intellectual or academic enough. When I was coming up, theatre directors were traditionally very academic, which wasn't my background.

But what's so amazing about being a theatre director is that you choose your family and you close the door. You choose the people you're going to collaborate with – the creative team and the actors – and you get into a room for six weeks. And nobody else is allowed in the room! Early on, I realised I could choose to close the door and only people who were part of the production were allowed through it. Some people found that a bit weird or cliquey, but that was the way I chose to work. And it meant that the pressure, the noise, the worries and the comparisons of the outside world were locked out. We could get on with finding our voice, finding our feet, being together and exploring in a safe environment. I use that term, 'safe environment', a lot. What I mean by it is that it isn't simply a place that is non-abusive, but an environment where you're allowed to make mistakes and look stupid, and none of what happens goes beyond those four walls.

Creating that place was so important to me. It was the only way I could deal with the pressures of being the only female or being the youngest or being a bit different or not being intellectual enough or whatever. I closed the door on all that and got on with the work with everybody else in the room – which was hugely enjoyable. We're lucky in that respect with theatre. It's not like a film set where anybody can walk on and off. In a theatre rehearsal space, there is literally a door and you can choose to close it.

ELLIOTT

You mentioned the greater number of female directors now working in the industry. Particularly at the start of their careers, how can they be supported? Is it a question of mentorship, opportunities to debrief together, directors noting each other's shows, or something more amorphous like friendship or emotional support?

A network of emotional support – that's always good. But actually, it's all about learning on the job. Most of the time, you don't want another director's notes, unless they're very good notes, limited in number and you can genuinely pick them apart in a friendly and collaborative way. What you need is your own work experience, full stop. And, crucially, the opportunity to fail as an experience. As a director, you need to fail a lot. And then get up and do it again. Nobody's brilliant from the start. You don't suddenly learn how to walk and then you're off. We're talking about a really intricate craft. Directors need theatres to invest in them as associates, not just give them a one-off opportunity. When I was an associate, I was given shows regularly – and half of them were terrible! I remember at one point thinking that I had created one show that was good, followed by one that was bad, and then back to one that was good. But it was all vital experience that helped me learn the craft. We need more theatre festivals, more fringe theatre, more grants, more associates – just more, more, more opportunities for these young directors.

Do you think being female has shaped your career as a director? Or has it been largely irrelevant?

I think being female has shaped me, full stop. It's a huge part of my identity and it shapes everything: what book I choose to read, what gallery I go to, what film I watch – everything. And so, necessarily, it has shaped me as a director.

Emma Rice

Stories of the subconscious and the skill of naughtiness

Emma Rice is an award-winning actor, writer and director who runs the Bristol-based touring theatre company Wise Children. She was the Artistic Director of Shakespeare's Globe from 2016 to 2018, but is best-known for her work spanning two decades with the hugely popular Kneehigh Theatre. Her creations, which include a significant number of adaptations, are famous for their exuberant visuals and joyful brilliance. Her work includes *The Red Shoes* (2000), *Tristan and Yseult* (2003), *Brief Encounter* (2007), *Rebecca* (2015), *The Flying Lovers of Vitebsk* (2016) and *Wuthering Heights* (2021).

'The most logical thing for my brain was dancing on the tables rather than reading at tables.'

Many of your most successful shows have been adaptations of already-famous films or books, so I wanted to start by asking what draws you to working on adaptations?

I'll start by saying that I've never had an original story come into my head – but I do have stories come into my head a lot, and they tend to be things that have been rattling around my subconscious in one form or another. I have a great belief that stories come to you when you need them. I see them as my soul food; there's a stock of them somewhere and they bubble up when required. One of the thrills of my life is seeing which stories start coming to me in my dreams and waking moments. Normally, they contain a personal resonance. Early in my career, I started thinking about *The Red Shoes* a lot, which was relevant to me because I was trying to make sense of my young marriage at that point. More recently, *Wuthering Heights* came to me, which was very much linked to my thinking about the current refugee crisis. Sometimes, the link is harder to initially fathom. I remember waking up and suddenly wanting to create *Steptoe and Son*. It took me a while to work out that was about family and entrapment, and my relationship with Kneehigh.

I think of myself as a detective. The stories I become obsessed with are the clues to what's going on in my subconscious and my life. They're personal, but they aren't mine. They're often from oral tradition or popular culture because I'm not very literature-based, but all of them are strange compasses to what my current state is.

When these stories come to you do you quite suddenly know: 'This is it, this is my next piece of work'? Or do they bubble away slowly in the background, maybe for several years, before you decide to create something from them?

It's sudden. I find that if you have an idea and it bubbles away, and then nothing happens, it tends to not be the right one. Things have to grow and develop, but I've got to a point where I can trust my instinct to know something is the right idea and to start work on it quickly. The ideas that don't end up becoming a piece of theatre weren't bad ideas, they just weren't the right ideas. Whereas the ideas that come to you at the right time, in the right moment: they're unstoppable. You can't shake them off, or let someone else shake them off. You simply have to create something from them.

When you're working on a story like *Brief Encounter* or *The Red Shoes*, where an iconic version of it already exists, how do you go about freeing yourself from that version so you can instead create something that is entirely 'you'?

I am very rigorous in not immersing myself in previous versions. For example, with *Wuthering Heights*, I can promise you I've never seen a film of it. A lot of people will always say, 'Have you seen such-and-such...?' when you're working on a story, but, for me, no good can come of seeing other people's ideas. Because if I love it then what's the point in making a new version? And if I hate it that just makes me a nasty person. Like *Wuthering Heights*, *Rebecca* was a rare instance in my career where I worked on a story that was originally in book form. And, in truth, I struggled to read Daphne du Maurier's book. The first half is great, but the second half is difficult and that was what provoked me to have a big idea. I thought: it's my job to make this fly.

I've got a natural arrogance that believes the only reason to retell a story is to bring something to it. For example, with *The Red Shoes*, one of the first things I knew was that the fight at the end was going to be to the death, but the girl was going to win, because in every version of *The Red Shoes*, she either dies or is sent into servitude. So

I was like, 'Well, what I'm bringing to this story is that this is going to be the bloodiest fight ever, and her feet get chopped off, but she is going to live.' Likewise, with *Wuthering Heights*, I decided very early on that I wanted this story told by the Yorkshire Moors. When I have an idea like that, I very rarely unpick those big decisions – because nothing would exist if I did. Other people can always knock down your ideas, so I don't knock down my own.

In terms of your process of adaptation, do you arrive at the rehearsal room with a completed script you've written, or do you prefer a process closer to devising?

I've been directing for nearly twenty-five years now and my process and the people I work with have changed over the years. With my early work, I would absolutely have the auteur's voice. I knew what I was doing, why I was doing it and I was very much guiding the room, but there would be a lot of devising going on. That's because, with the Kneehigh ensemble, you couldn't stop them devising if you tried. I also worked with writers a lot and I would have them in the rehearsal room with us. I would give them instructions like: 'Write me a piece about the Unloved.' Or: 'Go away and work on a fantastic fight sequence set to Nick Cave's music.'

But over the years, for better or worse, I've started to do much more writing. This is for two reasons. One: I've got better at writing, and I've worked hard at my writing. Two: the stories I'm telling have got a lot bigger. In the early days I was doing stories that could fit on four pages of A4. Whereas with something like Shakespeare, *Wuthering Heights* or Angela Carter's *Wise Children*, there's a lot of material, and you cannot ask a company to devise big pieces of work like that in five weeks. So, I do a lot of the work beforehand. I also work with new people more frequently these days, which means there isn't as much of a shorthand in the rehearsal room. But really, it's been a natural evolution underpinned by my own development as an artist and my ability to take my own writing seriously. In fact, it's only been in the last five years that I've taken my own writing seriously.

What shifted to make you do so?

Oh, just getting older. My life's been a series of surprises. I've always had a huge work ethic and great passion. But none of this was planned. None of it. I never planned to be a director. I never planned to be a writer. I find it excruciatingly hard. I'm very disciplined and concentrated in my work, but to actually sit down at a computer, it's physically painful for me. However, over the years, you dare yourself to do better, you get braver and so I battle with my own demons and do it. What results is joyful, but the process is fairly agonising.

It's all to do with confidence. I was a comprehensive-school girl who wasn't academic, so nobody had ever treated me – and I'd never treated myself – like I could be a director or a writer. The great thing is that everything's happened very slowly: I didn't come in and try to be a star director at age twenty-three. I've enjoyed every stage of my life: performer, choreographer, director and, now, writer. There's no rush in what I do.

Do those different bits of your creative career inform each other? I mean, did being an actor inform how you direct, and do your experiences as a director inform how you now write?

100%. It's all been so completely organic and an inseparable evolution. I'll always be an actor at heart. I profoundly understand how scary it is to be an actor and what the ask is. And, because of that, a lot of the processes I've developed over the years have been about creating an environment in which actors are able to be at their best. I'm really good at doing so precisely because I remember the desperate days of being an actor when you dreamt somebody would see you or would help you reveal your true capabilities. I understand the primal drive behind the car crash that is acting. I work with fantastic people, but I still think it's my job to get the best work out of everybody that comes into my room. Actors are, above anything, my absolute heroes.

And then, yes, the way I write is very theatrical because that's how I direct. I'm writing what I want to see on stage. I try to leave oxygen for the performers and creatives to breathe life into a piece. And I build a strong theatrical structure on which everybody can dance.

I'm much more efficient now – which is such a boring word! But if I do more of the slog part then everybody else can work at being exceptional and surprising on top of those foundations.

Could you talk a little bit more about how you get the best out of an actor? Do you have specific practices or routines you've developed over the years? Or are we talking about more of an atmosphere or belief thing?

It's definitely an atmosphere thing. And I would immediately caveat what I'm about to say with: who knows what actors say about working with me?! And, equally, my practices don't work with all actors. However, the first thing you need to do is to choose the right people, which I'm pretty damn good at. It's a cliché but I don't need to know whether somebody is good at auditioning, I need to have an instinct that they're going to work well with me for the next six months. In a way, doing an amazing speech is almost the last thing that concerns me. The next thing is something I've spoken about a lot: I try to remove fear from the room. Now, you can't entirely remove fear because it is in all of us. We all wake up pretty scared most mornings, and we're certainly scared in a theatre environment. Everything I do in the room, therefore, is about saying: 'You are free, you are welcome, you are respected and I delight in you.'

I'm not strict – people are late to my rehearsal room, and it does piss me off. But I tend not to express that because doing so doesn't gain you anything. That five or ten minutes is not worth what you lose by people feeling like they're going to get into trouble. We start each day by playing games and delivering the message that it's not about competing; it's about sharing naughtiness. I call it the skill of naughtiness and there are no repercussions to naughtiness, it's rewarded. We also always sing together, and it doesn't matter whether you're a good singer or not, there's lots of singing and we always dance together. And by that point, they're pretty knackered! So, anything they came into the room with is forgotten. We call it 'youth club' quite often: throw in the skills, throw in the fun. There's music all the way through rehearsals because there's nothing like the silence of a room to make people feel exhausted and frightened. In an ideal world,

I would use low lighting in the room, like I used to be able to do in the Kneehigh rehearsal space, so people don't feel literally exposed.

None of these are tricks, they're clear ways of saying, 'You're brilliant and you're safe – go for it.' I mean, not everything everybody does is going to be brilliant every time, but as long as nobody's ever punished or ridiculed, it doesn't matter. You're setting up a reward system, where people are brave, surprising, funny, exceptional, and then the room delights in that. You don't need to say that something isn't very good; all you need to do is make enough work that is good to simply let the bad ideas fall away. I work on a profound belief that criticism doesn't really help anybody. All it does is erode your confidence. And if your confidence is eroded, you're not going to reveal yourself. One of my most hated phrases in the world is 'critical friend'. I don't want a critical friend. I want a supportive friend. I want a friend who likes me and likes my work. We're all so critical of ourselves and I have to remember that about every actor who walks into the room, and myself. Every creative is their own biggest critic, nobody else needs to join in on that. So all you do say is, 'This is what's working, this is what's good, this is what I like.' And from those roots, the room takes on an energy of its own.

Have you ever had trouble creating that kind of positive atmosphere; for example, when a creative bond wasn't establishing itself?

It's certainly happened to me, but very few times. In fact, when you asked that question, the three times when I had struggled immediately popped into my head. None of it has ever been really ugly. We're all good people with the same aim: to make great work. But I do know that I can frustrate a certain type of actor. And that's the type of actor who likes to work on text and psychology and to have the script out in front of them. I tend to work from the story, so the text is almost the last thing that happens, which can frustrate some actors as they want something from me that I'm not good at giving.

Of course, I'm alive to an actor saying, 'Can we please talk about why I would say this line?' But my reply is usually, 'Well, you're welcome to change it.' Which, funnily enough, some actors find annoying as a response. I was working with one actor who approached me about a line that didn't make sense to them, and I said, 'Oh, you can change it.' And she said, 'No, I pride myself on being able to work with any script to make the line work, I just need your help doing so.' And I was like, 'Well, I wrote the script and I don't care. You're not honouring anything by adhering to the exact words: change it to what works for you!' But, really, that type of exchange is the worst those types of conflicts ever get. As I said, it's probably more annoying for that type of actor to work with me than it is for me to work with them. I'm not trained in that text-centric way. And I've never made any work that way. I don't have that psychological background, which I suppose is closely connected to method. But ultimately, I've never fallen out with anybody, and I always take full responsibility for hiring somebody. It's very rare but if it's a mistake, it's my mistake.

Is there ever a time in your rehearsal process where you do sit down at a table with the scripts out?

No, absolutely not. In fact, there was a funny moment when I first arrived at the Globe. Everybody had been very lovely to me and as we were going into rehearsals they asked if I'd like the room laid out for table work. I went silent for a minute. And I thought… 'I don't know what table work is!' Then I thought, maybe we dance on the tables?! But that seemed a bit odd, so I said, 'Table work?' and they said, 'You know, script work?' Then I was like, 'Oh no! I don't want any tables!' But I like how the most logical thing for my brain was dancing on the tables rather than reading at tables.

The reason I don't do that kind of work is because my background isn't through script. I find reading a script quite tedious and I don't want to waste three hours on it when we could have learnt a song or a dance in those three hours. But most importantly, table work is simply the place where you find out who's a good reader and who isn't, which is a completely irrelevant skill to me. All it means is that you've created a barrier in the room between the people who feel confident reading and the people who don't, which will have no impact whatsoever on their ability to perform or work with me. It also very unhelpfully establishes a sense of status in the room, whereby

people with more to say are more important than the people with less
to say, and you will never be able to fully break down that barrier once
it exists. In my room, everybody has an equal voice. It does not matter
whether you're playing Heathcliff or whether you're playing somebody
that moves a door, you have an equal voice.

Natalie Abrahami

The art of collaboration

Natalie Abrahami is a UK-based theatre, opera and film director. Alongside Carrie Cracknell, she was the co-Artistic Director of London's Gate Theatre from 2007 to 2012. Their joint tenure saw the tiny-but-mighty theatre awarded the Paul Hamlyn Breakthrough Fund for Creative Entrepreneurs. Preferring to work in a highly collaborative fashion with actors, playwrights and creatives, Natalie's previous work includes Samuel Beckett's *Happy Days* (2014 and 2015) and Arthur Kopit's *Wings* (2017), both starring Juliet Stevenson at the Young Vic, *Swive* [*Elizabeth*], created by Natalie Abrahami and Ella Hickson (Sam Wanamaker Playhouse, 2019) and *ANNA* (National Theatre, 2019), created by Ella Hickson, Ben and Max Ringham.

'Collaboration is at the heart of everything I do: It's what I love.'

From 2007 to 2012, you ran the Gate Theatre in Notting Hill with Carrie Cracknell. Why did you decide to apply for the position as joint Artistic Directors, and how did running the building together, rather than independently, shape that period at the theatre?

I met Carrie on the National Theatre Studio's Directors' Course in 2004, and we hit it off immediately. We had very similar thoughts about theatre and the people who inspired us. In particular, we were both very influenced by the international work and dance-theatre we were seeing as part of the Barbican's International Theatre Event programme. At that stage, we were keen to train and were applying to various funds and foundations to allow us to travel and to apprentice ourselves to international directors we admired. But despite applying we were not successful in any of them, and when the Gate job came up it seemed obvious to apply together to try these ideas out in practice. I think we just felt we were so in tune with each other.

It was the year the Gate was about to start paying the full Equity minimum and it was a gargantuan feat for a seventy-seater theatre to pay actors, given the low ticket prices and small box-office yield. Carrie and I knew, from looking at the application pack, that this was going to be a massive fundraising undertaking to reach these targets. Suddenly we would be running a three-quarters-of-a-million-pound operation when previously we'd only been in charge of our own student overdrafts.

With so much fundraising to do we wanted to work in a collegiate way to enable each other to also make work, so should Carrie be in rehearsals she wouldn't have to think about stakeholders or producing. We would be this protective membrane for each other, so that when one was directing they could just be directing. We also thought about putting forward a model of collaboration, in particular relating to directing and childcare, and how it would be really positive if either of us wanted to have a child, as one could be on maternity leave and the other would keep the organisation running.

But the surreal aspect of our application is that we didn't say any of what I've just said to you. We had these very rigorous interviews in which this was revealed, and I think it's all credit to the Gate's board, that they took a risk on us. We were twenty-six and twenty-seven, we hadn't made any shows… it was a real act of faith on their part. We didn't know what we were doing, at all. But we were very passionate.

Was running it together ever a challenge – were there times when your viewpoints clashed, or you each wanted to go in a different direction with a project? And, if so, how did you deal with those moments?

We worked very much in partnership, like a marriage. Joyfully, we didn't disagree, but we had a policy that if we ever did, we would never do so in public, so our team wouldn't have any confusion about how the leadership was working and we could resolve it between ourselves. But actually, it never came up because we were very in sync with each other and were continually checking in.

We genuinely wanted to support each other as creative makers. We've always given each other very tough notes. Really, really searing notes that come from a place of deep love and respect. Carrie and I had already been noting each other's work informally and we were excited about making that more formal. We would be each other's dramaturg, artistic director and producer. We established this very candid approach where we would say everything we thought needed to change. Sometimes, the other person would say, 'No, I love that bit! I'm not changing that!' For example, when Carrie made *I Am Falling*, I had very strong feelings that a song element in it should be edited out and she felt equally strongly that it should stay. That became a useful benchmark for us, so in the future we would reference that moment, which meant it was non-negotiable part of the piece and had to stay. That relationship has sustained, and I always invite Carrie to dress rehearsals and previews, and vice versa. Her notes are invaluable.

What was your vision for the Gate with both of you in charge – was there a particular ethos or approach to making theatre that you wanted it to be known for? And how did you go about creating this?

We felt very passionate about dance-theatre and adaptations of classics; giving opportunities to emerging playwrights, for example Sam Holcroft adapting *Uncle Vanya* and Lucy Kirkwood working on *Hedda Gabler*. These were projects that wouldn't ordinarily be given to playwrights until much later in their career. By offering these commissions early on the spirit was that of the Renaissance approach of 'imitatio'; learning craft from artists with greater experience, tempered of course with a large Gate dose of irreverence. To be in dialogue with Ibsen or Chekhov is wonderful, especially when also being given the freedom to make massive departures.

We also worked a lot with emerging designers. We followed the Linbury Prize for Stage Design and would give designers the opportunity to use the space however they liked. One of our board members referred to the Gate as a 'magical shoebox', and it was that transformative aspect of the theatre to which we were drawn.

We wanted to create a sense of freedom for everyone to be their best creative self. We didn't have money, so creative freedom was what we could offer.

From the perspective of an artistic director, when you're working with new and emerging playwrights and creatives, how – on a practical level – do you support them and inspire them to feel genuinely confident?

I think first and foremost artists need the opportunity to make work. That is how we learn. Whenever we were meeting emerging directors, writers or designers, there was so much energy and appetite, but the question was who was going to give them their first break. Our theatre was called 'the Gate' but we wanted to make it the opposite. We wanted people to know we weren't gatekeepers, we were welcoming creatives and giving them as many opportunities as possible. What we could offer was the time and the creative backdrop, and as much of Carrie and myself as was useful or needed, to support the directors and designers on that journey.

When you come across a playwright whose work you'd like to direct, for example with Ella Hickson, are you responding to a sense of connection with the playwright themselves – as in, 'I could work with Ella' – or is the connection all about their words and a desire to put their play on the stage?

I think there is a lot of affinity involved. My collaboration with Ella started when I read a play of hers in 2009 and I met her, as I met many writers, with the view to her doing an adaptation of a classic for us at the Gate. That didn't happen, but that's where our relationship started. I guess I was drawn to meet her initially by reading her writing and then, having met her, I was compelled to work with her by her personal qualities: her intellectual curiosity, passion, synthesis of ideas and global political thinking. I think it always starts with the writing, because often you don't know who the person is before you've read anything by them. Later, you might decide you don't want to work with them on that specific play, but know you want to make something together. So you keep in touch, keep up to date with their work and, one day, find another way of collaborating.

When working on a play by a contemporary playwright, how closely do you like to have them involved? For example, do you invite the playwright into the entire rehearsal period, or do you have them there for a short period and then ask them to leave?

I will eagerly spend as much time with a playwright as they can give. I invite them to all auditions, rehearsals and creative meetings. I think there is sometimes a period in rehearsals that is quite hard for writers.

I try to prepare them for this by explaining how there's a time when we are getting to know the text and it won't sound very good, but you need to have faith in your words and believe we will get there rather than thinking, 'This sounds so awful, I must change it all!' The writer can choose to stay away if they'd prefer but, from my perspective, I'd love them to be there all the time because they can be helpful with making decisions by telling us how they saw a scene or what they imagined the tone of it to be.

And in terms of the other people you'll be working with closely, do you go into the creation period of a new show with a very clear idea of what you want the visual aesthetic to be, or do your designers take the lead?

I tend not to give visual references. I might name a sculptor or an artist, but I try to be very respectful of the designer's visual domain. For instance, when I was working with Vicki Mortimer on Samuel Beckett's *Happy Days*, I wanted to make a show that felt very contemporary – like it could be about a woman who lived next door to you who was in an awful situation. I didn't want to stage it in someone's home, but I wanted that to be the concept. I also wanted to have a climate-crisis narrative, so there was a reason why Winnie was buried up to her neck later on in the play. Vicki and I both shared photos of places we'd been to that could be hostile environments for Winnie and they were all remarkably similar in their terrain.

I try to provide the creative team with the impetus for why we are telling this story now. I then see how they respond to that and we work very collaboratively from that point onwards.

How do you decide that a designer is going to make a good creative partner and that your imaginations will be aligned?

I think it's similar to what I was saying about Ella Hickson and other playwrights: first you read the work and then you meet the writer. I first saw the work of Tom Scutt – whom I've now worked with on multiple occasions – at the Linbury Prize exhibition and I was staggered by it, so I invited him in for a meeting. I'm always curious to get people to talk through their portfolios as a way of understanding what makes them tick and what their inspirations are. With Tom, I found his brain, his intellect and his excitement about the world fascinating, so we made a show together almost immediately. I often say to the directors I mentor that the designers they meet might not have a portfolio yet, but you might, for example, have seen a show they did on the fringe and liked it. I suggest going to art galleries together, going to the theatre together, starting talking about what you think work is, and what work you want to make. That's how Carrie and I started collaborating and that's the model I use with my collaborators now.

Do you think you've made any mistakes when working with other creatives on a show?

Absolutely. Collaboration is at the heart of everything I do and if you don't have a good synergy, it's incredibly lonely. On productions where I haven't quite connected with my designer or my lighting designer – whichever collaborative relationship hasn't quite gelled – the lack of it is heartbreaking and the work is poorer for it. That's why I try to be more and more fastidious when deciding with whom to work. I ask other people what it was like to work with them, and I ask the person I'm meeting what they've liked when working on other shows, who they've worked really well with, and what they've found difficult. These are significant relationships to embark on, and exercising due diligence is key, so I reference and I ask people to be articulate and honest about themselves. Every time I don't get it right I have to look at what I did wrong.

When I was an associate director at the Young Vic, I was often asked what the theatre could offer those who were no longer 'emerging' directors. So, I set up Debrief Dialogues, which is where a group of directors meet to talk confidentially and solve problems among ourselves – and often those problems are connected to collaborations that aren't working. Directors find themselves in complicated situations all the time, and it's difficult to learn from them unless you analyse them with your peers.

Whenever I run a workshop for emerging directors, I always say, 'Rise with your peers.' I unequivocally feel that there is space for everyone, and that support can be vital when you encounter problems and don't know who to talk to about them because you're no longer training.

On the occasions when you've developed a particularly close relationship with an actor – I'm thinking specifically about Juliet Stevenson on *Happy Days* and *Wings* – what was the working relationship like there?

This is the joy of long-term relationships. In 2005 I was lucky enough to be the recipient of the James Menzies-Kitchin Award for Emerging Directors – I actually won it at a point where I was thinking of giving up directing. I decided to stage two Samuel Beckett plays, *Play* and *Not I*. But I was terrified of directing them, terrified of the Beckett Estate and terrified of not being able to talk to the writer. So I wrote to lots of people who had made Beckett's work; people who had either been in his shows or directed them. Nobody got back to me. The only person who did was Juliet Stevenson, and she invited me to her house and showed me all the notes she'd made on both *Not I* and *Play* – and exercises that she'd done to help her performance.

Then, of course, it felt lovely to be able to offer her *Happy Days* in 2013 as a continuation of this first encounter nearly a decade earlier. *Happy Days* is a scary show to make because Beckett puts the director in the role of the torturer: asking the performer to be incredibly uncomfortable for hours every day. I was very candid with Juliet, asking how we could make that work for her. We also knew it was going to be a big mental achievement and very tiring to learn. Because of that, our process involved lots of tea breaks, naptimes and cake.

We wanted the nature of being trapped that we were depicting on stage to feel very embodied. So, one day we went to Regent's Park and buried Juliet in a leaf pit. I wasn't asking her to do anything I hadn't done before – I had gone a week earlier and done it myself. The idea was that Juliet would be able to experience what it was like to be really constrained, which would make it feel different when doing it in a theatrical context.

With *Wings* there was a lot of training involved for the aerial component of the show, and Juliet was so up for that idea because she knew we had this shared language and support system, and that I would protect her through a process that was physically and mentally challenging.

When you are working on a play that involves a 'big name' actor who the storyline focuses on – the way *Wings* focuses on Juliet Stevenson's character, Emily – how do you make sure there is a sense of unity and parity within the whole cast, so that people don't feel like: there's Juliet Stevenson and there's 'us'?

You'd have to ask the actors because I don't know if I succeeded. But I was very conscious of those dynamics, and I think if you can be conscious of what your potential problems might be, you can work to solve them.

Like a parent, as a director you want to meet everyone's needs, and the needs of somebody who is going to be hanging aerially for seventy minutes are different from those of a performer who doesn't have to do that. Yet you can all do the warm-ups together and you can be a collective.

On that occasion, I tried to find as much time as possible where we were working together as an ensemble. My memory is that it was an incredibly happy company. Everyone had different challenges and everyone was trying to support each other. Anna Morrissey, the movement director and a long-term collaborator of mine, would often work with one set of actors workshopping an upcoming scene while I was working with Juliet on the aerial moves. Then we would meet and share what each group had been doing. I think there was a lot of love and respect in those rehearsals.

With *ANNA*, the parameters of making a binaural sound piece in a hermetically sealed glass box for six weeks in a rehearsal space without natural light, meant that we knew there would be huge demands on the makers and performers of the piece. We created our own code of conduct to help us prepare for the obstacles ahead and enable everyone to feel supported. It was a collective list that included principles of mutual respect, all ideas being welcome, and also embraced the particular sonic and experimental spirit of that project. One of my favourite mantras that emerged was, 'We are sound performance artists and the glass box is our instrument.' This one helped us navigate gnarly moments when we had to make decisions that prioritised the sound focus of the piece rather than a character choice.

The Rehearsal Room Code principle proved so useful I now do it with every company, and it is fascinating how each group of people bring all their previous experiences with them to enable them to be clear about what they require to make their best work.

Where does your own ambition feature within the network of collaborations your work involves? Did you ever – or do you ever – entertain urges to make the kind of work which foregrounds your status as a director, like making Natalie Abrahami's *Hamlet* or developing an aesthetic immediately identifiable as the 'Natalie Abrahami aesthetic'?

I was very lucky that my first show was annihilated by the press and I think that taught me to have a strong sense of artistic growth based on my own assessments and the views of those whom I really value, rather than relying on outside validation from the critics. The fact that I chose to go back into the directing world meant I could inure myself and feel, 'I'm on my own journey.' I have a clear sense of: What does Carrie think of my work? What does my partner think of my work? What does my brother think of my work? They are on this longer journey with me.

I want to make sure I'm challenging myself to be more rigorous, more experimental, more creative, or more immersive. But I'm on my own trajectory.

There was an occasion where I used a gauze-effect technique in one show and then used it in another. Ann Yee, a brilliant choreographer collaborator of mine, whom I made *Rusalka* with, called me out on it. I was so embarrassed that Ann had spotted that I had repeated an idea and I vowed never to do that again. It also made me realise that I don't want to have a signature! I don't want people to be able to recognise my work; I want to make the right choices for each particular piece.

Emma
Frankland

Using (or not using) lived experience

Emma Frankland is a performer, writer, artist and director who was once described by a critic in *The Stage* as 'the punk-rock angel of your dreams and nightmares'. She is the author, performer and creator of the *None of Us is Yet a Robot* series of performances, which are published in book form by Oberon Books. Her work frequently explores the concept of transformation via natural materials and processes. As a director, she has worked on Rachael Clerke's drag-king punk gig *Cuncrete* (2016), the dance-theatre hybrid show *Republica* (2019) and *Galatea* (2023) by John Lyly.

'It's all about an invitation, rather than an expectation, to share.'

Many of your previous shows, which you've both performed in and authored, are based on or heavily utilise lived experience. So, I wanted to start this conversation by asking you about the whole idea of 'lived experience' in theatre, both in terms of its power but also its potential limitations and challenges.

Absolutely. It's a concept I've been thinking about a lot recently because it relates closely to the project I'm currently working on as a director. *Galatea* is a play written in the 1580s by John Lyly. It pre-dates Shakespeare and is one of the inspirations for *A Midsummer Night's Dream* and *As You Like It*. But in Shakespeare's plays, wherever queerness is encountered it is resolved in a heteronormative way – things often end in gay panic – whereas in Lyly's work things remain very queer and, moreover, trans characters and gay characters, and their love, are celebrated at the highest level. Indeed, the goddess Venus, the goddess of love herself, both allows and celebrates queer love. It's a remarkable play that says loads about the history of queerness and the existence of trans people in theatre for generations. The production uses a huge company of fourteen actors, plus an extensive crew, and one of the things I was keen to do with the casting was to cast people who would not consider themselves 'actors'. I also wanted to not just cast people who we are used to seeing represented in classical English theatre, i.e. straight cis white people, or at the very least, straight and cis people. So, I've been bringing artists to the project who have their own practice and/or lived identities that reflect the characters in the play.

I also wanted to find ways for the acting company to then bring their lived identities to the play, even if the characters as Lyly wrote them didn't explicitly have identities that overlapped with those of the performers. To give an example: there is a character called Peter who is described as Black. For me, it was vital to cast a Black performer in the role as there are precious few characters who are Black in theatre in general, let alone in the classics. Which means, in this case, lived experience was – in a straightforward way – essential. However, the question then arises of how much pressure there is on the performer to bring their lived experience into the rehearsal room. For me, it is key to have a system wherein you say, 'Your lived experience is welcome and valid – but equally, you don't *have* to bring your lived experience.' It's about putting agency in the hands of the performer, rather than in the hands of the director or casting director or writer, as it has historically been.

Then, to give another example, we have characters whose race and identity is not specified, which has given us a beautiful opportunity to be informed by the performers in the company. So, for instance, one of the performers we're working with identifies as a Deaf queer non-binary Scottish-Thai person, and they're playing a character who is not listed as any of those things, but for the purposes of our play is all of those things because that's what the person playing them is. It's been amazing to chat through the process with them. They've said that at times in the past they felt they could maybe bring one of their identities to a role, but never all of them. But once again, that's only on the days when it feels comfortable for them, or in the manner that feels safe, and is led by them. Interestingly, we've found that bringing those qualities to the role has enabled us to unlock lots of further potential for that character. It's all about an invitation, rather than an expectation, to share.

In terms of your own experience as a performer of work based on lived experience, did you find there were days when engaging with that felt like too much or too heavy? And what, in those instances, did you do?

Yes. We often see artists making work that speaks about the places in which we are most marginalised or the experiences that have been the most harmful because, understandably, those are the things we want to heal and within them are the lessons we want to share or make urgent. But the question hanging over it all is, 'How safe is this process? How safe is it for the artist, for the creative team and, in the end, for the audience?' Part of that question is about consent. For example, if you're sharing potentially triggering information, are an audience receiving adequate communication about whether or not they're going to be called on to participate? When it comes to the safety of the performer, for my part, I've had the good luck to create work surrounded by people who cared for me. When I was first making pieces around a decade ago, I worked with the theatre-maker Rachel Mars, and there were several occasions where we were working to a performance deadline that was tied to our funding, so there was quite a lot of pressure to meet it. However, there were times when Rachel said to me, 'I don't think this is for them [the audience] yet. I think this is still for you.' And what she meant by that was that I was still in the process of figuring out what the language of the performance was and what my own identity was in the piece. Then, when we later got to the point of sharing the work with other people, the things in it didn't feel super-hot any more. That's often been the case when I'm working on something: by the time I get to performing it for an audience it feels current but also something I'm, by that point, comfortable sharing.

But that isn't always the case for everyone. For example, I'm currently working with a Black trans masculine neurodiverse artist who's made a piece about their experience of police violence and being over-policed as a Black person. That content doesn't get less triggering for them to perform – it doesn't recede or become resolved. In instances like this, it becomes vital to think of ways they can be cared for in the creative process and during performance runs. This could include how the production budget covers therapy costs or facilitates rest time. Or if there need to be certain processes put in place to help them after each performance.

In the example you gave of working with Rachel Mars, how did you know the moment was right for you to share the work with an audience?

I think part of that is just having that question present in the room. That way, it's being thought about and it means you have permission to always go back. Even if you've performed it once, it doesn't mean you're bound forever to perform it again and again if it doesn't feel right. The show, ultimately, does not have to go on. There is huge power in realising you can say no if something doesn't feel appropriate.

And when you're in the role of director, as with *Galatea*, what processes do you put in place to keep performers, who may be going through similar journeys with lived experience and making theatre, safe?

I will start with a super-important caveat: I don't have all the answers. With *Galatea*, I'm working with a big team, and we are constantly learning. The thing I'm most proud of in this process – which has so far lasted over seven years – is that, as a team, we're always checking back in with people at each stage and ascertaining what felt good and what we could have done better. The show uses British Sign Language and spoken English, and a proportion of the company are Deaf, which means they have some specific, clear access needs. But we've also used that as an opportunity to constantly be learning a little bit more and offering a little bit more support. We've been able to do so only because of the generosity of those Deaf artists who have shared with us what hasn't gone right, and through us listening and then actioning that. The message, really, is to trust the people who are telling you what their needs are – and asking people what they need is something we've asked the whole company. It's a question some people will be happy to answer – some will have the document ready to go – whereas others will have no idea, or some idea, or feel unsafe asking. That means you need to broker those conversations in a bespoke way. It also comes back to time and money and, often, making work at a slower pace. It sounds strange, but don't make the finished, staged piece your end goal as a company. Make your model of success one in which you consciously looked after your company and your audience. If you do that, the play will probably be pretty good too.

We've talked about the challenges of making work with links to lived experience, but is there also something cathartic or healing about making and performing work of this kind?

I think catharsis is really important. I did a performance of *Rituals for Change* that was for a trans-only audience. I was terrified about whether they would like it and whether it would feel like I was speaking out of turn. But it was one of the best experiences that I ever had performing the work because of how cathartic it was to be in a room full of people with similar lived experiences. Instead of feeling like I was doing the job of explaining, it felt like I was doing the job of connecting. In recent years, I've also performed my show *Hearty* a lot. And, increasingly, I find that one of my most difficult works to perform because the global situation around the topics the work discusses has grown much more difficult. I also feel a weight of responsibility that comes from performing words that have been given to me to share by other trans people from around the world. Those are stories about difficult things, up to and including genocide. But I know it's important to share, and oftentimes the response of a trans audience member will be that these things are things we are all feeling. *Hearty* is very expansive, fiery and explosive, and it's great to have a space to rage and to share all that.

Do you think there is something particularly powerful for an audience about a work that's been made with reference to lived experience?

I don't know. There is power in seeing someone's true lived experience, but I also believe in the craft of performance and the craft of theatre. The lie is also really strong. Just because we can tell true stories doesn't mean they are more effective than sometimes telling fabricated ones. Audiences don't necessarily need to know if something is fact or fiction to connect to it.

There's also an important question of ethics. I've previously worked with Selina Thompson, who made the incredible show *Salt*. There was a period of time when that was a very difficult show for her to perform because she's a Black British writer and artist, and the show speaks about her experience of grief, ancestry and colonialism. There came a point where that piece was being booked by theatres and there was a conflict over the benefit for audiences of seeing it versus the difficulty of performing it. One solution was that, for one run, the part was recast, so someone who was not Selina was playing Selina in a true story. For some people, the piece 'didn't count' when someone other than Selina was playing Selina. But what kind of attitude is that? Are you saying that, as an audience member, unless you see true pain it doesn't count? That feels very uncomfortable and violent as a response.

I believe there is space for the craft of theatre and acting, and for the truth to come through that. I'm personally at a point where I'm interested in returning to fiction, partly because I'm fed up – to put it mildly – of only telling my own story. I want to support other people being on stage and, moreover, I want to give other trans performers the chance to be expansive and explorative without having to mine their own traumas. With *Galatea*, we've got a play that speaks about the migrant experience, acceptance of outsiders, the right to protest and other hugely relevant topics. We don't have to be hurting ourselves to get those messages across.

Picking up on that point about caring for performers and their stories, on your website you have a guidance document available for download, that theatres and companies can consult when working with trans performers or telling trans stories. Could you start by talking about how that document came about and what the initial impetus was behind creating it?

I am very proud of co-authoring that document and I send it out to theatres almost on a monthly basis. It came out of a multi-day workshop I co-ran as part of the Stratford Festival in Ontario, Canada. The company is like the Canadian equivalent of the Royal Shakespeare Company in the UK, and they were doing a series of workshops investigating the concept of the canon, because their main reason for existing involves performing the Shakespearean canon. The workshops included ones on the canon from a Southeast Asian perspective or a Black Canadian perspective or an Indigenous perspective. I was invited to lead on the canon from a trans perspective and I asked to bring another person with me to run the workshop because I didn't want to be representative of the entire UK trans experience. So I ran it with Subira Joy and six trans and two-spirit artists.

The idea of the 'trans canon' or 'What is the trans perspective on the canon?' is a difficult one because there is no trans canon! The 'trans canon' is about erasure, violence, moments of acceptance, and lots of films and plays and books written by cisgender people about traumatic things happening to trans people, plus trans people recounting their trauma in solo monologue shows. Which meant it was hard to get on board with this idea of 'What is the trans canon?' whilst also recognising that there is, of course, a whole history of trans performance that has shaped where we are now, for better or for worse. We also found that, more than some of the other workshops, people found ours relatable, because everyone has a relationship to gender whether you are trans or not.

Anyway, after working together for almost two weeks, we started to think about where all this conversation was headed. It was great that a specific organisation was making some enquiries but, really, what was that going to lead to? We didn't want to end this passage of work without creating some kind of legacy. So, over about two days, we drew up this document which is intended to offer some guidance for situations in which an individual trans or two-spirit person is working in a big, theatrical system where it is often very hard to advocate for yourself. This document would advocate for them.

When you send it to theatres, what is the response typically like?

Theatres love it because it's doing a lot of work for them. Everyone I send it to says, 'Oh my god, this is brilliant, thank you so much!' Whether they then do the things suggested is the next question, of course. But it's important to at least be putting these things out there. It goes back to what we spoke of near the start: when you're asking people to bring their lived experience to a production, extra care is required. And what does that care look like? If you've got one trans person in a show and that person is having to advise you on the script because it's been written by someone who doesn't have that experience, what are you doing, above their existing wage, to recognise that? Are they getting a credit line in the programme? Are they getting paid? Are they being offered counselling? Was it consensual or did you ask them because they were the only trans person in the room? Would they have preferred you to bring another consultant in? Even people who feel they are doing things well are often still taking advantage and it's hard to push back on that, especially if you're an actor or a creative who has already committed themselves to making a show.

If there was one thing you could pick out from that document that you feel is the most important point you would like theatres to take from it, what would it be?

I think the most important point in that document is to recognise that extra care is required when people have multiple intersecting marginalised identities. There's a danger that, with increased trans awareness and people wanting to work with trans people more, white trans experience becomes the default trans experience. Yet there are so many ways in which white trans people are much more advantaged and respected than, for example, trans people of colour or Black or Indigenous trans people. The key thing in that document is about recognising there are extra things you would also need to consider when working with any Black or Indigenous company member, but these are amplified for trans people of colour, and Black and Indigenous trans people. There's an amazing book by Sabah Choudrey called *Supporting Trans People of Colour* that's a lot more thorough than the guidance document. But I think the key point is that organisations should start by recognising they need to take extra care.

Indhu Rubasingham

Cultural specifics and universal appeal

Indhu Rubasingham became the Artistic Director of Kiln Theatre in North London in 2012 and oversaw its transformation from its former incarnation as the Tricycle, before announcing she would depart the venue in 2024. She is a multi-award-winning director whose credits include Lolita Chakrabarti's *Red Velvet* (2012), which transferred to New York and the West End, and Moira Buffini's *Handbagged* (2013), which also transferred to the West End, New York, Washington, and received a national tour. She frequently directs works by playwrights from across the world in productions that highlight both the specific and the universal aspects of different cultures.

'Right from the beginning of my career, I've been determined not to be defined by others.'

In preparation for this interview, I spent some time trying to summarise what your 'thing' as a director is. I was trying to work out, for instance, what characterises an 'Indhu play' or what's immediately identifiable about your work. I decided instead that, aside from working consistently with living playwrights, what characterises your work is an amazing diversity in genre, setting and form. Do you agree with that as an assessment?

I think you've hit the nail on the head. Right from the beginning of my career, I've been determined not to be defined by others. When I was starting out, I was aware that, being an Asian woman, there were a lot of expectations, perceptions and presumptions. All of which I wanted to challenge. I think that decision has informed me as an artist and a director, as well as immense curiosity and a passion for narrative. At Kiln Theatre, the work has ranged from Florian Zeller to Zadie Smith to first-time playwrights to comedies and adaptations. And, as an artistic director, I've maintained that type of variety so that even if an audience member doesn't like one part of a season I've programmed, they can come and see something else later on that month that they might like. The common denominators across the work I direct and the work I programme is that it needs to, firstly, be of the highest quality possible and, secondly, to offer those watching a different perspective or different world view.

In connection with that 'different world view', your previous work spans a great variety of different cultural settings and geographical locations. When you're working on a play based around a specific

set of cultural reference points, which are different to your own background and experience, how much preliminary research – and of what kind – do you do into that culture?

As much as possible, in many different forms, but what's great is when you're working with a living playwright, the best research tool is right there: the playwright. I'm not being glib, it's that they've nearly always done a huge amount of research themselves, or the play is based on their own lived experience, and they know their stuff – it's their words.

Really though, this is what I love most about the job: it allows me to learn about and enter different worlds. That's not something you get with most other jobs. Whether it's different cultures, different locations, different countries or different time periods – anything that's not my lived experience allows me to enter another place and another person's perspective. In terms of research, one strange thing I've noticed is that when you're researching something, suddenly the whole world seems like it's talking about it too. So, for example, when I was working on *The Great Wave* by Francis Turnly for the National Theatre – a great, huge play about North Korea and Japan – just as we were finishing auditioning and about to go into rehearsals, Donald Trump met with North Korea's leader, and it was everywhere in the news. Obviously, that was an actual coincidence of events, but I think when you're working on something you also just start seeing references to it everywhere.

By the time I go into a rehearsal room, often I will have been researching and thinking about a show for around two years. As an artistic director, that research often involves things the assistant director has worked on and researched too. It's also not simply a matter of reading books. 'Research' can mean listening to music or talking to people who have experience or knowledge of whatever the play is about. For example, with *The Great Wave* we didn't have anyone from North Korea in the cast, but we had someone from North Korea, who had escaped the regime, come in to talk to us all during the rehearsal period. The cast can also unlock other aspects of a play through how they say a line and the experiences they bring. I'll also frequently have enlightening, revelatory conversations with a lighting designer or a set designer which will totally inform my understanding of the play I am working on.

When you're working with a living playwright on a script, do you see the playwright themselves and the text as being the ultimate source of research? By which I mean, do you see those two sources as containing the real essence of what you need to know as the director and as better than, say, any reference book or resource?

Absolutely. The playwright is the source of the play. They have got the ultimate research material and have spent more time than anybody with the material. However, there are times when a writer's closeness to or expertise on a topic might mean everything, or some details may be opaque to an audience. When a writer is writing from the perspective of lived experience, your outside perspective as the director can make them see things they might not have considered otherwise. When someone knows a topic or a situation so well, they don't always think about the things someone who isn't familiar with it would need to know. It's important to look at a play from as many different angles as possible: lived experience, outside experience, academic experience, and the visceral, sensual and environmental experience – the smell, colour and feel of the world depicted.

Does your research into place and culture involve travelling to different places?

I've done so once or twice, but nowadays I usually can't afford to spare the time. Early on in my career I was working on a Ugandan play by a Ugandan playwright, and I was very privileged to get British Council funding to go to Uganda and to travel around the country with the writer so he could show me everything he was talking about in the play. That was fantastic. I also had the opportunity to go to Japan when I was working on *The Great Wave*, but I didn't have the time – so my assistant director got to go to Japan instead! I also worked on a play set in Bradford, where the playwright was from, and we went on a fun trip for a few days around town. Again, that was so useful. It's wonderful to get to go to the place you've been researching and thinking about so much, but getting the opportunity to do so is often very hard.

Taking *The Great Wave* as an example, when you're putting on a play that is set in Japan but you're presenting it to a London audience – most of whom won't be Japanese – is your directorial focus on bringing out the universal aspects of the story (things we could all relate to and understand), or are you more interested in emphasising cultural specificity and uniqueness?

In a way, both. As a rule, I believe that the more specific a work, the more universal it becomes. A really good example of this is when I directed Dael Orlandersmith's *Yellowman*. That play is set on the Gullah Islands, off South Carolina, and is written in a very specific dialect. The title, *Yellowman*, refers to light Black skin. I remember talking to one artistic director and they told me it was an American play that wouldn't work for UK audiences, partly because – they thought – we don't understand shadism in the same way as the States. They also pointed out that it's a play that's extremely culturally specific and uses a very particular dialect. It's not a widely known dialect, even in the States, and to perform the play well we needed to get that dialect correct. We were opening the play in Liverpool. The cast and I worked hard on dialect and on the specifics of the play's world – and it absolutely landed. Every night, predominantly white audiences, full houses, standing ovations: it just worked. And that taught me that it was the specifics of the play that released the universal emotions and humanity of the piece. It's through exploring specifics that we're able to engage with human emotion – and human emotions are always universal. Had we worked to generalise or deliberately universalise that particular play, we wouldn't have been able to release its power and passion, both of which came from this very specific experience.

That said, it can sometimes go the other way. I've worked on several plays by Anupama Chandrasekhar, a playwright based in Chennai, India. I remember reading a draft of her first play. There were lots of bits of exposition. I asked her why these bits were in the script and it turned out it was in response to a dramaturgical note she had been given by someone else who had told her that she needed to add these parts to make the play more accessible – it's actually one of the best notes I've ever given a playwright. I asked her, 'Why don't you write the play you actually want to write?' And I asked her to make it more specific – add more Tamil words, more specific cultural and linguistic references. She wasn't initially keen but, for me, it was the specifics that gave the play its flavour and colour, and its universal appeal. However, when I started work with the same playwright on a different play, I actually did suggest we do the opposite! I felt there were moments where, if the audience didn't understand that particular word or thought – if it was too alien to them – then the meaning behind the moment would be missed. So I asked her to strip some parts back. It's a fascinating balance when you are working on plays and playwrights from different cultures and countries. We have to be careful with how we land an idea or a thought, so we don't miss that universal connection. But, on the whole, I do veer much more towards being as specific as possible.

Often when I'm watching a play in a totally different dialect or cultural setting, I'm struck by how easy it is to understand what's being said even when I'm unfamiliar with the cultural setting. Even when someone uses a bit of slang or a word from another language, most of the time you know what they mean without overly trying.

Absolutely. It's the context, isn't it? I remember directing a play that contained a lot of slang relating to North London. Friends of mine were saying how very, very specific that play was because these words would only be said by someone from the area. I didn't know these words, but I felt completely confident in directing it because I understood the context. As an audience you don't need to know the slang and language if you understand the context and, once the actors are delivering the lines, the intonation and the intention contain so much of the meaning.

Talking of confidence, was there a particular point in your career where you started feeling confident in yourself as a director, both with making the kind of decisions you just mentioned, and more generally?

It's funny, because obviously I feel confident as a director now – but you never lose the frickin' fear. I was thinking about this on my last show.

I was like, 'I'm so anxious. I'm so tense. I mean, seriously, is this what it's going be like every single time?!' But then I realised: this is my life. I'm always going to be anxious, and I'm not just talking about as a director. I'm always going to be anxious working on a show if it means anything to me, and if it stops meaning anything to me, then I'm obviously not in the right job any more. But it does take a lot out of me.

I remember when I was directing Molière's *The Misanthrope* and a critic said to me – funnily enough – 'Oh, that has all the hallmarks of an Indhu Rubasingham production!' And I was like, 'No, it doesn't! I don't have hallmarks; I'm serving the play!' But it was weird because it made me realise that, actually, as the director, you do put yourself into the play, even when you think you don't. Your energy, your sensibility, your aesthetic, it's all in there somehow. Even though, at the time, there was me sort of going, 'I'm an invisible director, you can't tell I'm present!' That moment made me realise that no director is invisible in the work and everything you work on lands inside you in different ways.

There was also another moment when I realised that my experience as a director had given me a kind of integral confidence to be bolder and go with my instincts. Knowledge doesn't necessarily make you confident, whereas now I know that, for me, inspiration can come from anywhere at any point. It might be in the shower, for instance, and I now know to trust that instinct and not to overanalyse that or get hung up on where the source of that idea comes from. What's also interesting is how your process diverts and evolves in difficult circumstances. When I first started being the Artistic Director of the Kiln, I found it really hard. But combining all the different challenges has made me develop my directing process. Being even more limited for time led me to start storyboarding the whole play with the creative team prior to going into rehearsals, so when we're in the room we all know where we are. That's been so helpful to my process, but it only came about as a technique through pressure and stress.

In terms of that pressure and stress, what do you do when it's all over? Do you shake off that emotion once a show has come to completion with any particular ritual or routine?

Oh, no – the day after press night I'm really low! I need to go under a duvet forever. It's very emotional. You've been investing in this living, breathing thing for so long and now it's been released into the world. And it doesn't matter if it's gone brilliantly and been received as a 'five stars best thing since sliced bread' show, it's always the same. It's always, 'Oh god, I don't know who I am any more.' And, 'Nobody needs me any more; this thing I've created is happening without me.' There's always a bereft moment after a show opens, always. So, I need to find a way to let off steam in some way. Going to a spa would be good! I need to sleep. I need to be in the dark for a while and I need to work out who I am again. It takes a few days to recalibrate.

Debbie Hannan

True accessibility and the reality of having bodies

Debbie Hannan is a writer and director of theatre and film, born and raised in Edinburgh. Known for highly visual shows with a punk aesthetic, they have created work for the National Theatre of Scotland; the Royal Court and Bunker Theatres in London; Manchester Royal Exchange; Tron Theatre, Glasgow; and the Traverse Theatre, Edinburgh. From January to July 2022, they were the Acting Artistic Director of Stockroom and are currently an associate director at the National Theatre of Scotland. They are an active advocate for disability rights and reforms within the theatre industry, both on and off stage.

'I'm a fan of the "no excuses" approach.'

Shortly after the coronavirus pandemic shut down the theatre industry, there was a lot of discussion around 'accessibility' and 'inclusivity', with the aim of changing the industry for the better once things opened up again. You've spoken about accessibility and disability quite a lot, so I wanted to start by asking you how – in a practical, applied way – you make your rehearsal rooms and productions accessible to people with all kinds of needs?

On the first day of rehearsal, the first thing I say is, 'We're going to be in a room where we acknowledge the reality of having bodies.' What that means is you can say what you need, and you can express what's going on with your body privately or publicly. I also speak from the point of view of someone with an invisible disability who needs certain accommodations and acknowledgements of what's happening with me and my body on different days. The thing I would emphasise is that, once you open up that conversation and a new level of acceptance around bodies and their needs, you automatically acknowledge the reality of having a brain and mind as well, because that aspect of ourselves just comes with our physical beings. So neurodivergence and mental health also become part of the room.

The other thing I mention right at the start is what I call 'the squidge'. The squidge is the thing that exists around almost all identities that have an aspect to them that is difficult to ask about, or that people feel awkward addressing – perhaps because they're unsure of the correct language to use, or they're afraid of offending someone. So, I think it's massively important to confront the fact the 'squidge' is going to exist and work to find ways through it, rather than doing the clichéd British thing and avoiding talking about anything awkward.

It's also worth noting that 19% of the working-age population in Britain is disabled, which equates to one-in-five people. Placed in that context, you realise that the conversation should be about more than 'representation', it's actually about erasure. Because the one-in-five statistic means that, if you have a cast of five, one person should have a disability. Or, in a creative team of five, one should have a disability – and if they don't, then you are erasing a type of person from the world by not having them present. There are fewer disabled people working in the theatre industry because of all the obstacles and the relentless issues around establishing a career in this line of work, but I'm a fan of the 'no excuses' approach. So, while it can be true that it's hard to find people working in the industry with disabilities, it's still unacceptable to only have people on your team who aren't disabled – both things can be true at the same time.

Where mental health is concerned, how do you go about having conversations with your cast and crew about that, and what practical things do you put in place to underpin that?

To start with, I think literally raising it in the room is important. However, I've also worked with companies who have a Mental Health First Aider. If that's a possibility, then it's a vital resource to utilise, although it's often not something you have access to at an early career stage or when you're working for very small companies or theatres.

As a director, I borrow from what is known in teaching as 'trauma-informed pedagogy'. Loosely speaking, I run a 'trauma-informed rehearsal room' and that involves things like acknowledging the potentially harm-laced power dynamics of the whole rehearsal room or theatre industry. So before we even get to discussing the content of the play, I will acknowledge that I am 'the director' and that implies a certain power dynamic and so, to address that, there needs to be a whistleblowing system outside of me so that if, for example, you're uncomfortable with something happening in the room or something connected to the play and you don't want to bring that up with me, you also know you can go to the stage manager or the producer or someone else connected to the company. The aim is simply that everyone feels they're able to express themselves if something is not working.

Another thing is making sure mental health is understood as something that must be managed, and often needs time or resources to help with that. If, for example, someone has an access worker, I will make clear – from auditions onwards – that they are welcome in the rehearsal room. It's useful to also acknowledge the intersectional nature of mental health, that it doesn't happen in a vacuum and it crosses over significantly with neurodivergence. I also address the fact that, ultimately, I need to make a piece of work, but your mental health needs shouldn't prevent you from being a part of the creative team and working in the theatre industry. Just to be clear, I don't position myself as some kind of guru-doctor who can help cure people, I just try to create a room with parameters that help to make sure everyone is able to be there and make their best work.

Where content is concerned, I'm very aware I seem to keep doing plays with such difficult content – like, mega-triggering! Which means that, right from casting when I send out materials for auditions, I'll make sure the casting director knows to include a trigger warning. In a slightly more intangible way, I also try hard to create an atmosphere in the rehearsal room where whatever comes up in response to the content of a play is seen as important. I know some directors like to specifically discourage or exclude 'anything personal' from conversations about the play, but, in reality, that's not how humans work. For example, when I read a play I will often think, 'Oh, god, that is just like my feeling about x or my experience of y.' And, of course, when actors are embodying characters or designers are thinking about spaces, it's natural for personal reflections to surface and that's fine. I make clear that nobody has to share anything they don't want to, and I lead any discussion that takes place so that it's useful and relates back to the work in an applied way.

I find it funny when people freak out about people getting emotional or crying in a rehearsal space because I'm like: we work in theatre! Big feelings are part of our world! But it's also important, as the director, to keep tabs on people's emotional vulnerabilities and bring things that are shared back to the work itself, because we're ultimately there to make work – that's what we do. I want everyone to bring their full selves to the work, in a safely held way, and that includes the audience as well. There are so many stories about directors approaching traumatic content and just thinking about the 'drama' of the sexual assault, or whatever the moment is, without taking responsibility for how that affects the audience and the cast performing it. Rethinking how something like sexual assault is staged can include things like how it's lit and what is shown, but it can also include providing trigger warnings or information on related helplines to the audience. All these things can get labelled as soft, 'snowflakey' stuff, but actually they're about letting people come to the theatre and enjoy it. If your show is reliant on shocking someone with one individual, horrific scene, it's probably not the best show.

On the whole, how do you find those kinds of conversations around mental health are received by cast and crew? Are people quite receptive to opening up and sharing things, or do you find that some are a lot more reticent?

Absolutely, it's a real mixture. Everyone is on their own individual journey with their disability and mental health, or even with their body if they're non-disabled. Everyone is in a different place. I've found that people who have a visible disability – for example, wheelchair users like Saida Ahmed, who I worked with on *Little Miss Burden* at the Bunker Theatre in 2019 – are like, 'Great! Now I can tell you all the pragmatic things I actually need to tell you, like when I need my carer and when I'm going to be late because of taxis arriving and why I can't use the DLR easily…'

But with other people, it's such a personal journey in terms of what they want to reveal. And that links to privilege, because when you reveal something vulnerable about your body or mental health, it can feel like you've dropped in status. That's certainly a debate I've had myself, about whether I should share my needs or hide them because, most of the time, I have the privilege of 'passing' as a neurotypical, non-disabled person. As the director, it's in no way my job to pressure anyone out of the place they're in; my focus is on setting up a world where they can advocate for their needs if they want to. I also hope that, by loudly shouting about my own needs, I'm setting an example and helping people feel comfortable and happy to do it themselves.

It's also worth saying that this doesn't just apply to disabilities and mental health. I've also found that running this type of room has allowed, for example, actors on their periods to be able to say, 'Yeah, I'm exhausted today, I've got loads of cramps and no energy.' And I'm absolutely cool with that, it's so weird that a bodily reality that applies to about 50% of bodies on the planet isn't usually acknowledged! Yet if you know something like that, and can work with it rather than against it, it actually makes the work so much better. It's why accessibility is so important in the first place. We can get very lost in lofty, moral conversations about the philosophy behind it all – and send a load of tweets accordingly! – but actually it's just that theatre is meant to engage humanity, and if you don't exclude anyone from that, your work will be much better because it will be more varied and creative.

You mentioned working with Saida Ahmed, who has a visible disability, on Matilda Ibini's *Little Miss Burden*. Could you talk me through a few of the practical arrangements you put in place in the rehearsal room and the production itself to work with her needs?

I'll start with talking about rehearsing and planning the show, and then the content of it. With a show like *Little Miss Burden*, you need to have producers who are on board with receiving a different list of demands – and luckily we very much did. If you only want to work to a fixed template, it won't work, which is true of any show. You should always tailor a show individually according to what it, and the cast and crew, need. But I'd specifically recommend getting an access meeting with your producers and venue as soon as possible. Arrive with a list of questions, things like: Do they have an access officer? What's their version of a relaxed show (because everyone's definition of a relaxed show is slightly different), or what is their history with staging accessible shows? It's a difficult conversation to have, but you should also address the issue of money because you may need to push for a bit more budget to be allocated on these things. It can be common to get told, 'We don't have the money for that.' And while the theatre industry isn't swimming in gold, that response isn't always totally true. It can be a case of moving funds around a bit and reallocating money, or it can be about thinking very creatively about how you're using money and coming up with new ways of distributing it.

Really pragmatically, rehearsal space is a big deal. You need to consider things like travel arrangements: Can everyone easily get to and from the venue, and what can you do to make that easier for them? You also need to think about things that could easily seem insignificant, like the length and timing of bathroom breaks. A quick dash to the loo is different if someone has to go up three floors to collect a special key to then use the one accessible toilet which, again, is in a different part of the building. If you're working with people who have care packages, as both Saida and the playwright, Matilda, do, then you need to factor the care-package timing in to the rehearsal schedule. That might mean that, for instance, you planned to do a 10-to-6 day, but it turns out that can't work for all your crew and creatives, and you need to shift things around and only do 11 to 4. Then, as the director, you can also think about how to schedule in smarter ways and, say, think about whether you have other actors who can use the last few hours of the day to rehearse a different scene, or if you can use the remaining time for another purpose. You might also want to consider if you're going to need a scribe or other assistants in the rehearsal room at certain points, and how you are going to make sure they are available when you need them to be.

Another thing to think about is blocking, because learning blocking can be different for people with different bodies. I mean, it actually varies between actors anyway because some, for instance, only learn blocking once they've internalised the script and others only learn the words once they've got the blocking. However, I've found that neurodivergent and dyslexic actors can have a different relationship to blocking and, if you've got an actor with a mobility issue or visual impairment, you have to be even more conscious of how you set up the space so that, when you transfer to the actual stage space, they've had the best preparation to get there. On which note, it really, really helps to get the set and props as early as possible. That can involve a lot of work from crew and producers, but it massively helps with the overall readiness of the play.

Then, in terms of content of the show, I wanted to have a visual dramaturgy that, to quote Taylor Mac, allowed us to 'dream the culture forward'. I wanted to create the world on stage that the play itself is trying to create, which is one where a disability is not an obstacle. The social model of disability teaches us that it's not a person's disability that's the obstacle, it's the way a society views and responds to that disability. I wanted to make a space where being a wheelchair user didn't prevent Saida from going anywhere on stage. I also wanted it to have a lot of style and flair. From the design meetings with designer Helen Hebert, we came up with a space that looked sort of like a nineties playground with mad colours and levels and loads of ramps. When Saida first came onto the stage she literally screamed in delight because she'd never had a set design that wasn't just a flat floor, and ours had three levels and she could whizz around all of it.

You said that the Bunker team were highly responsive to those conversations, but have you – without necessarily naming names – had experiences where people were not responsive, and what did you do in those scenarios?

Yes, I have very much had that experience. It's hard. I think when I've previously sort of bumped into a producer, the fact is that this 'stuff' just isn't part of their world. It's new for them and, to them, it seems like another thing to add to their to-do list. What I've done then is make it clear that all this is rooted in the reason I make work which, in turn, is why they have me there as a director. And if they don't want someone who's going to consider access at every level, then they should have hired someone else. That's what they're getting with me and the benefit to them is an expanded audience, which is what theatres want and frankly need. So, there's no loss to this being one of their considerations – it's a good thing. And in terms of the 'inconvenience' of it, well, that's the squidge: this wedge between the perceived inconvenience and the cost. I make clear that we're not at the forefront of a new empire.

For decades now, people have been innovating how we make theatre, and setting up brilliant practices and putting out open-source resources. There are whole campaigns, like We Shall Not be Removed and Disability Arts Online, and artists and companies like Birds of Paradise and Graeae. These are companies that you can go to, and they will speak to you about what's what and what works best. They've been through the 'inconvenience', they've been through the years of working out what the best system is – and they'll help out. I think working harmoniously with producers and theatres is about making sure it doesn't feel like a singular effort this one producer or one building is going to have to make that is brand new and stressful, and they're going to get horribly shamed on Twitter if they don't do it – it's not about that. It's about connecting to a whole different set of audiences and being part of a lineage of people who've been doing that advocacy and that pragmatic work for such a long time.

A few years ago, we did another interview together where you spoke about your own experiences with an invisible disability and how, early on in your career, you didn't want to mention it to people or ask for the things you needed, like a particular chair or saying when you were severely fatigued. I wondered if there was a particular point in your career where you felt emboldened to advocate for your own needs? And is that something people are now receptive to?

Yes, they are actually – which is great. But it's a good question, and it's so complicated. I've got Ehlers-Danlos syndrome, which is a connective tissue disorder and means I have a host of complicated interconnected issues that can affect my mobility and energy levels, and means I dislocate joints frequently. However, to the naked eye, I probably appear completely non-disabled. As an assistant director, I basically made the decision to sacrifice my health for the work – a decision that was influenced by also being someone who came from a working-class background in Scotland and wasn't set up to easily succeed in the London theatre industry. I thought that I would just work myself to the bone in order to succeed.

All that work I did as an assistant, or early career director, for free or on small projects, that's all added up to me being able to do the brilliant things I do now where I can advocate for myself. But during that early stage, it was really hard. I sit here with the privilege of being someone who can pass as non-disabled, something I know got me jobs I otherwise wouldn't have been given. But I definitely made myself very unwell, physically and mentally, as a result.

The shift happened when I really hurt myself. I was a trainee director at the Royal Court, and I snapped a ligament in my ankle. I was working on a brilliant play called *Teh Internet Is Serious Business* and I fell on the tiniest bit of set – just a little lip – but I rolled my ankle and it snapped and dislocated. It was so extraordinarily painful. I got wheeled out of the Royal Court, which was my theatre home, on this emergency wheelchair and then I had this terrifying meeting with a doctor where she talked about the potential of where this degenerative condition could go, with how run down I was. And I had to go: Okay, I've got to change my lifestyle significantly, because I've been throwing myself against the wall of work over and over again.

Yet despite all this, I think it actually took maybe another two to three years of reckoning with what I need to do, and what I can do. And shifting the picture of what work looks like and what being a director looks like. We work in an industry where 'being a director' means working through every break, every lunch, every day. You're the first one up and the last one to leave, and there's no Equity protection for you or your hours. You're sacrifice-able, but you're the leader, so you can't complain about that.

Anyway, it took a few more years but eventually I started asking for things. I started with a chair – which is quite embarrassingly small, really. I was at the National Theatre of Scotland, which was a big moment for me as I had started my career there, and ten years later I was invited back to do a show. During the R&D, I had to ask for a different kind of chair, and I was so worried I would sound like some kind of diva who wanted a throne, but actually they were totally great about it, very accepting. If they hadn't been I would probably be telling a different story right now. They were like, 'Sure, what kind of chair? What else will you need?' And now that I am the one in control in the room, I make sure I ask those same questions to everyone I work for so they can get what they need.

When I came to work on *Little Miss Burden*, I realised I could never do that show with integrity and honesty without admitting my own needs as part of the process. That was a massive shift because it took me away from feeling like this is something I've got to conceal and potentially be embarrassed about – I had quite a lot of internalised shame about it – to being something that is wonderfully part of how I do things and why I do things, and actually made my relationship with that playwright and cast so much better.

The sad but true answer is that when I got the power as a director to set up the rooms I was in – which you don't have when you're assisting or when you're on a low-budget thing – I was able to make the changes I needed and other people needed. As I said, I think I had a lot of internalised shame about being disabled and also being queer and working class, but I also had this fucked-up version of privilege where I could hide all those things. But actually, the more I have leant into those elements of myself, the more people seek me out to direct those stories, or do workshops on access with other directors, which is so fulfilling and important.

I think that's a massive deal: learning to lean into your 'thing' – the thing you think you should hide. This might mean – I'm trying to think of a delicate way of putting this – pushing against an older generation of theatre-makers' ways of thinking, which include, for instance, working through lunch. I no longer work through lunch, I can't work through lunch because I have to press pause and rest. And because if I, and everyone, has a lunch break it will make the afternoon so much better. There is this fetishisation of the life of a director where you never stop working, and if you personally can and want to emulate that then go for it. But I can't and I won't – and, if anything, it's going to just make my show better if I take a thirty-minute break.

Lynette Linton

The Queen of Cuts on working carefully with playwrights

Lynette Linton is a playwright and director who became the Artistic Director of the Bush Theatre in West London in 2019. Her work as a director includes a five-star production of Lynn Nottage's *Sweat*, which premiered at the Donmar Warehouse in 2018, before transferring to the West End, and the critically celebrated *Blues for an Alabama Sky* at the National Theatre in 2022. She also collaborated with actress and director Adjoa Andoh on *Richard II* at the Sam Wanamaker Playhouse, the first-ever production of Shakespeare on a UK stage created and performed entirely by a company of women of colour. Under her direction, the Bush Theatre has been a beacon for new writing, particularly by playwrights of colour, including the world premiere of Waleed Akhtar's *The P Word*, which won the 2023 Olivier Award for Outstanding Achievement in an Affiliate Theatre.

'I'm holding their baby in my arms…'

Before working widely as a director, and then becoming the Artistic Director of the Bush Theatre, you started out as a playwright – and have continued to write plays alongside directing them. Did you intend to work as both a writer and director?

I accidentally became a director! I started off thinking I was an actor, which I think is because that's the performing arts profession you see growing up, on telly and things – particularly if you're not from a theatre background. Directing doesn't seem like a 'job' until someone actually explains it properly to you. I also thought I might become an author, because I loved reading novels so much and had started writing while still at school. I then went on to do an English degree and, afterwards, joined the National Youth Theatre, still thinking I wanted to be an actor. But it was at the NYT that I met the actor and director Rikki Beadle-Blair, and he basically changed my life, because he saw something else in me – something other than being an actor.

He gave me a free ticket to the new-writing festival he was running at Theatre Royal Stratford East, which was my local theatre. I went along and, almost immediately, I thought, 'Oh my days, I need to write a play!' So, I wrote a play called *Step* which was first on at Theatre Royal Stratford East and then, after being rewritten slightly, toured to schools. It was when I took a step back from the piece – originally I was also performing in it – that Rikki asked me if I'd ever considered directing. I was like, 'Umm… no!' And he replied, 'Well, you're basically directing now.' He saw this thing in me before I saw it in myself. So then he invited me to shadow him and be in the room when he was professionally directing. I learnt so much from him. He kept encouraging me and sent me on courses, and eventually I started to think, 'Okay, maybe I am good at this. Maybe I *am* a director…'

Do you think your experiences as a writer have influenced how you now direct?

100%. As a director, I'm incredibly text-led. Again, I get that from Rikki – people call me a mini-Rikki Beadle-Blair! – and from other experiences assisting directors. But I think the thing that my own experience as a writer has given me the most is how my practice is all led by the text. In the rehearsal room, we do loads of text work. I always start with a table read – because, seriously, table reads are magical – and then we'll do facts and questions, and then we unit it, using Stanislavsky's technique for breaking down a scene into smaller chunks to show how a character's intentions change over time, and we try other activities that delve into the text. I don't want the environment to become overly intellectual, so I throw in lots of jokes and dancing and movement as well, but without that deep-dive, I cannot truly understand that text.

I'd also add that the text itself can change right up to the last minute. I'm constantly asking questions about plays, even if they're already published, like, 'Is that line working? Could we move it? What does it really mean?'

I think being a writer has also influenced how I work with other writers. For me, the playwright is at the centre of the room, because it is their space and their work. They are welcome into the rehearsal room whenever they like, and we need to establish a relationship where we can both speak entirely honestly to each other. The idea that someone could write something and then not be welcome in the room makes no sense to me.

When you say the text can change up to the last minute, does that mean you are particularly bold with making cuts?

I cut everything! This is where I am a 'mini-Rikki' the most, because cuts are the best thing in the world. They really help. But they can't be done bluntly. And this where your relationship with the writer is so important. You can't just go in on day one and say, 'This isn't working!' They need to be able to trust you and you need to trust them. In order to do this, you need to think carefully about the language you use and the way you approach making any potential changes. Ultimately, this play is their baby, and you need to be careful about how you talk about their baby. For the first few days, you need to spend some time thinking about how everyone is using language and making sure there is a lot of respect present in how everyone is giving notes. Establish that and you should then be able to have the most honest conversations.

I'm a very honest and – I hope! – approachable person. So a playwright should feel able to come up to me and say, 'Lyn, this is not working.' And then I'll be like, 'Yeah, it's not, is it? Why isn't it?' And then we'll have the conversation we actually need to have. You shouldn't ever be pretending like you've got it together all the time when you're in the rehearsal room, whoever you are. And cuts are part of those honest conversations that should be able to take place. I will say things like, 'Do you mind if I try and cut this – and if it doesn't work, we will put it back in?' It's always framed as a negotiation, so the writer doesn't feel bombarded with cuts coming from me or from the actors or from the movement director or anyone else. We need to make sure that space feels sacred to them.

Going back to your dual experience as a writer and a director, including as a writer who has had other directors stage their work, has that led to you consciously thinking about what it is that a playwright wants from a director?

Absolutely. I think it comes down to care. It's also about negotiation and thought-time and being able to honestly say, 'Maybe I'm wrong.' But most of all, it's about care. I was recently doing some dramaturgy on a new play and the playwright said, 'I think I need to cut this scene down.' And my literary manager, who was also there, said, 'Oh well, Lynette is the queen of cuts.' Which, you know, is a pretty cool name: Queen of Cuts! But I never actually think of them as 'cuts'. I think of all of it as care, and I think of all of the reasons why it's beneficial for that part to go or be changed. Like I said, I'm holding their baby in my arms. If you've worked on something for two or three years, and it might be a representation of you or your family, or something else you feel strongly about, it doesn't work to have someone come in and just go, 'That's not working. Trash that bit.' That's horrible. So along with working from a place of truth and honesty, I also work from one of care to make sure people, including writers, feel safe and heard in the space. I've taken that through to how we work at the Bush more widely. We are a very care-led building.

In terms of your work as the Artistic Director at the Bush, do those experiences you've already discussed – being a writer and working with writers – also influence the types of plays you're attracted to programming?

Yes! And, once again, this is partly down to Rikki's influence. I'm very focused on what I call 'story vs theme'. If there isn't a story that you can boil down to, say, six bullet points, then it's probably not going to be something I'm excited about. Unless, perhaps, it is doing something exciting with form that I haven't seen before. Above anything else, I am very story-led and that's how I run the Bush. I'm interested in character and story, and how you use those vehicles to captivate an audience. I place this concept – story vs theme – at the centre of my writing workshops. People often want to write about incredibly important, big themes like sexism, racism, homophobia and transphobia, and they often pitch ideas by saying things like, 'I want to write about sexism.' But sexism is a theme, not a story. You need to ask yourself what the difference is between a university lecture on sexism and a play about sexism. The answer is that a play is a story, and it has a dramatic drive. The lecture is a lecture and a speech is a speech, but a play is different.

I used to have these conversations with Rikki and the writer John R. Gordon where they would be like, 'You're only talking about theme. Your character is just getting on stage and doing a monologue about how they feel about the world. That is not a play.' The type of plays I've always wanted to write – and programme – are ones where you are totally immersed in the story and then suddenly: bam! Something totally unexpected about it hits you. I need to know what the action of a script is before the themes get put on top.

We've talked about your route into being a director, but what made you also want to take on being an artistic director?

I wanted to be an artistic director because I felt that in order to really make change happen, I needed to be in a building. So that's why my work as an AD involves a lot of community work, and why a huge part of my practice is working with young people. One of the projects I am most proud of since starting at the Bush is the setting up of two youth theatres. I feel constantly inspired when I am working with young people, and these were the first two ever young companies that have been delivered in-house by the Bush. I try to pop into those sessions at least once a month because I get so much energy from being around these incredible people. I think the young companies get to the heart of why I wanted to run a building. Theatres are institutional – and that isn't ever going to totally go away. They are funded by the Arts Council and the government and other bodies, so the challenge is in how we make sure they become comfortable places where anyone can walk in and want to be there.

Theatre has always, to many people, felt elitist and like it's only for a certain type of person. And there's still so much work needed to change that. Personally, I want to see more of that work happening in connection to curriculums in schools. I can sit in the Bush and watch a play with a young person, yet I know they would still feel uncomfortable going into most other theatres. Lots of things contribute to making a theatre genuinely accessible: the ticket prices, youth theatres, community work, the prices at the bar and food we serve, and so on. My mum never went to the theatre growing up and still doesn't, if I'm honest. And when she came to the Bush when I first got the job she was like, 'How much is the cappuccino?!' I'll never forget it because her daughter now runs a theatre and she was like, 'I'm not paying that for a cappuccino.' So one of the first things I did here was bring in one-pound-a-cup Yorkshire Tea at the bar, because whenever you walk into a space and are like, 'Ugh, I'm not paying that for a packet of crisps…' or whatever, you don't feel the space is for you. All those kinds of things are important to me.

When I was younger I would find myself sitting next to artistic directors in various spaces and I couldn't see anyone else who looked like me. I didn't see women of colour, I didn't see women from East London, I didn't see women who sounded like me. I was like, 'Yo, where are we?' So when the job at the Bush came up, I remember looking at it and going, 'Ah, if only this had come up two years from now, then I would be ready…' You know, that sort of feeling. But my friend told me that I had to apply. And originally, I thought I would be too young or too this or too that. But finally I thought, fuck it. I applied. And I got it. Which is still mad to me, sometimes, because it genuinely is the best job in the world. The last few years, with the pandemic in particular, have been extremely hard. But I still feel like I'm incredibly blessed to be here running this fabulous building.

Vicky Featherstone

Weathering disruption and finding new writers

From 2013 to 2023, Vicky Featherstone was the Artistic Director of the Royal Court Theatre in London, often considered the 'national theatre of new writing'. Before this, she was the founding Artistic Director of the National Theatre of Scotland and, prior to that, the Artistic Director of Paines Plough. Across all these roles, and her own directing, she has maintained a fierce dedication to staging new writing and nurturing contemporary playwrights. Her time at the Royal Court was characterised by unapologetically politically engaged programming and the championing of playwrights and directors from backgrounds traditionally marginalised in British theatre. This interview was conducted in 2021, whilst Vicky was still working at the Royal Court.

'It takes a village to discover a new writer.'

As the Artistic Director of, firstly, Paines Plough, then the National Theatre of Scotland and, at present, the Royal Court, you've had three major roles at organisations known for their commitment to nurturing contemporary playwrights. Was it a conscious decision, early in your career, to focus on new writing?

I went to the University of Manchester and, while I was there, I threw myself into studying Drama. Through the conversations taking place there, I realised I very much enjoyed learning about existing, classic plays – the Chekhovs, the Ibsens, the Shakespeares and so forth – but, really, I am most excited by theatre being made now. In particular, I was interested in the politics, with a small 'p', around who was writing these plays, who was seeing them, what they were able to say and how they were able to reflect the world that we live in. One of the books that was very popular in Manchester at the time was John McGrath's *A Good Night Out*, which was very much about how you use theatre to tell a story that wouldn't otherwise be told.

What I was interested in wasn't called 'new writing' at that point – I think that label came later as an Arts Council funding thing. But I was very interested in all the contemporary playwrights I read as part of the course, and it wasn't until I got the job at the Royal Court that I realised how basically all of the plays that we read – the Caryl Churchills and various other writers – had all premiered at the Court! Which was very interesting. Anyway, when I left university and knew I wanted to be a director, I was only ever interested in finding a living writer and working with them. I don't think that was a conscious decision, there was just a very natural journey towards that point.

In terms of plays that respond to the 'now', when you programme work as an artistic director, are you looking for plays that respond to a zeitgeist, or are you looking for plays that will, in time, create a zeitgeist or help set an agenda?

It depends. At Paines Plough, which I ran for seven years, and at the Royal Court, the focus of those companies is very much on the voice of the playwright. So, in both those roles, the emphasis has been less on telling a playwright to write a play about a certain topic or issue, and more about speaking to playwrights and seeing what they want to write about – it's very writer-led. There will be times when you feel like, for example, we should be programming more plays about the climate emergency or whatever, but really, you're not totally in control of that. You're only in control of deciding which writers to commission, not what they write.

At the National Theatre of Scotland (NTS), it was slightly different. I set it up from scratch, so we weren't inheriting a particular way of working with writers. NTS's job was to tell the stories that needed to be told and sometimes that meant an adaptation, sometimes that meant a classic play and sometimes that meant something brand new. There, it felt it was much more possible and right to ask a writer to write about something specifically. *Black Watch* by Gregory Burke is the big example of that, which I commissioned for the NTS when it was literally just me working, alone, in the office. I realised there was an important story to tell that was going to encompass Scotland's relationship with England and the then-current politics of the Iraq War, and I specifically commissioned Greg to look at that story. Similarly, at the Royal Court, we commissioned Michael Wynne to create the verbatim play *Who Cares*, which came out of a collective decision that we needed to programme something about the NHS. But, on the whole, it completely varies depending on the writer and the situation.

Both from the perspective of programming plays as an AD and selecting them to direct yourself, do you think you are now looking for something different in scripts than what you were looking for earlier in your career?

I actually don't think I am. Because the thing I look for in a script is to be surprised, which means discovering or being introduced to something I couldn't have known or thought before. Often that's connected to the form that a writer uses, because I'm very drawn to plays that play with form and are slightly impossible. By which I mean, I haven't directed many plays that are set in tangible or possible places. A lot of the plays I have directed combine a mixture of political specificity with imagination, and I'm interested in how those two things sit together.

I don't think, however, that I would have been able to answer that question until very recently. It's looking back at the plays I've directed that I see that I've been drawn to the ones with that quality. I've directed very few plays that are issue or identity-led. I'm more compelled by metaphorical ideas of universality.

Returning to your interest in working with contemporary writers, how do you – as a director and an artistic director – really discover new writers and new works? I mean, obviously there's the practical gains of working at a theatre with a literary department and an open submissions policy, but how do you *really* ensure that it's not the same people, or kinds of people, coming through the same channels?

This sounds a bit obvious, but it takes a village to discover a new writer, or someone who can become a new writer. We could look, for example, at Jasmine Lee-Jones who had her debut play, *seven methods of killing kylie jenner*, performed at the Royal Court. Jazz is an amazing playwright and human being, and I feel so proud that it was through the Royal Court that she got her first big play on, and I think she will continue to change the world with her writing. When we look at how that play came to make it to the stage, Jazz had about ten different relationships or interfaces with the Royal Court that enabled her to get to that point.

What you often see with new plays or new playwrights is that somebody meets somebody somewhere at a workshop, and they think they are interesting, and they say, 'Have you thought about this?' And then the playwright responds and sends something relating to that question and then that gets handed on and read by someone else who also champions them, and so on. It's very rarely the case that somebody magically writes a play on their own in their bedroom, sends it in, it's read by a reader, it goes into the script meeting, it's commissioned, and it's put on. That does happen, but it's very rare. The discovery normally happens thanks to a team of incredible, passionate people who care and desperately believe in the discovery and the nurturing of new-writing talent, who seek that talent and that potential and hold it to its best.

It's about people working in participation departments, being in writers' groups, being in lots of different things where they hone their craft and their confidence. And at each stage of doing these things, the writers lose a little bit more of their imposter syndrome, because they feel held within a house. The older I get, and the more I think about it, I realise that finding new writers involves an incredibly complex – sometimes accidental, sometimes deliberate – series of Venn diagrams.

Do you think you've got better at finding people as your career has progressed?

I haven't got better at it. But the people I work with are amazing, and the places I work at, and the people I work with, are better at it than I am. As the saying goes: you should only ever work with people that are better than you. One of the gifts of working at the Royal Court is that our mission is so clear and so pure. And it's never changed since 1956. So even when things are really difficult, and really complicated, the focus just returns to: Who is the writer? What's the right thing for the writer? Are we discovering the writers?

And that mission brings everyone who works in the building together. I genuinely think that we only have people working at the Royal Court who absolutely believe in that mission in their core. One of the most exciting things to see is the way people champion the talents of others, which I think is rather gorgeous. And that can be someone who is the newest member of staff, or someone more senior, and they would be listened to if they said, 'I've read this and it's great.' Which is why it's important that a theatre's staff is as diverse and broad-ranging as possible. That way, it's not just a question of what my personal taste as the artistic director is, or what the plays landing on my desk are, it's about ensuring there's a massive series of different conversations happening.

Do you maintain a big focus on the writer and the script once you get into a rehearsal room? Specifically, do you start off with, or prioritise, table work?

Yes. I feel that the process of a rehearsal is a sort of jointly shared journey towards a deeper understanding of a play. And that journey ends when we put it in front of an audience and see how they receive it. I actually love the process of going through all the different stages to get to that point.

I never feel that I'm coming into the room with a 'thing' or a 'vision' that I'll give to the actors and creatives. For me, the point of initially sitting around the table is to start to come to a common understanding of what the play is, and it's particularly important that everyone is involved in those conversations. We start doing that together, before we stand the play up, so that we are all responsible for what we're creating.

After that first bit of table work, we move on to unlocking the movement of a play. I'm continually fascinated by the idea that you very rarely need to block a play. Part of that is an obsession about where or how movement is unlocked. Usually, it's unlocked from the internal architecture and psychology of the play, and that directly relates to how a play then fits onstage.

So, my first thing, once we stand it up, is to start working in a very free space – no props, no entrances, no worrying where the audience will sit. It's all very unliteral and focused on how all our bodies are in this place. We then start trying loads of different things out, just very natural different movements and then reflecting on what we, and the other performers, are doing. The interesting thing about working in this way is that the performers start to own the movements in their bodies because they're the ones who have come up with it. So, when you then say, 'Okay, so this is where the front of the stage will be or, this is where the audience will sit, or the door to the room will be', they still hold a lot of their original freedom in their bodies. And learning blocking becomes almost unnecessary because they've discovered the moment almost entirely organically.

You mentioned putting the play in front of audience and seeing their reactions. Part of that audience will, inevitably, be critics. When you programme new writing for a space like the Jerwood Upstairs at the Royal Court and that work is, often, experimental or politically radical, do you speak to the playwrights – especially, say, if they're a younger writer and it's their debut play – about being reviewed and the potential for those reviews to include some negativity?

Yes. I think it's important that you're all clear about what the endeavour is – and you hold on to that. So, one of the things I do, and the Royal Court does as a whole, is to try to build up resilience in a playwright before a play opens.

It's about believing in the integrity of a play and making sure that belief is shared throughout the building. We always say to playwrights that we do not judge the success of a play on the reviews. The success of a play is that we made it together and it is on in front of an audience. You can never really take away the difficulty of a bad review for a writer, but we can hold fast to the view that they do not sway our opinion of the work that we put on. And you have to work hard in an organisation for that to genuinely be true, because people often say it doesn't matter when it does. Whereas, at the Royal Court, I genuinely do believe that we don't judge things in that way. Evidentially, it will be easier to sell out a debut show if it gets a whole bunch of five-star reviews. That's a practical fact. But it doesn't mean that play is any better or any less good than any other. There are so many other ways to judge the success of a piece of work and we work hard to help playwrights believe in the value of the thing that they've written, and we've programmed.

Do you have any personal practices when it comes to reviews of shows you've directed? Do you read them straight after press night, for example?

Well, I read them with my glasses off, at a distance, so I can't *quite* see them…! More seriously, the thing about reviews is that I value and respect people who write about theatre, because that is a beautiful thing. So I have a complicated relationship with them, because people have given their whole lives and made a whole career out of going to the theatre every night, and then sitting down and writing about it every day. Which is kind of amazing!

But then, on the other hand, your relationship with the work that you make, as the artist, is very fragile. And what I've learnt as I've got older is that I need to protect that relationship with the work that I make. Because, really, it's all that I have. Years of care and artistry go into creating a piece of theatre, and when your relationship with that work is broken, it's a very, very painful thing. What I've realised is that I have to protect the endeavour of the piece of theatre that I originally believed in, and the group of people that came together to tell that story because we believed in it, loved it, and thought it was extraordinary. We, as a group, never set out to make something that was shit; we didn't set out to upset a critic. We set out on this journey together with absolute belief in the potential transformation this work possessed.

Because of that, we have to protect each other from the things that can change that feeling, and that 'thing' isn't the same as someone simply not liking a show. It's the thing that happens when a review tips over into being toxic. When that happens a review can change the physiology connected to how you feel about a work, and that is very, very destructive. A really bad review can make an artist feel shame, because so many people have read it and you're embarrassed by that. As we know, shame is such a destructive emotion – and once you feel shame, it's so hard to let that feeling go. It can wane, but it never completely disappears and you never really feel the same thing about the work again. So the relationship with reviews, for an artist, is very complicated.

That reminds me of something another director said to me, that it's almost impossible to separate 'you' from your work.

No, that's right. You can't because you bring everything that you have at that point in time to it. And you don't set out for it to be bad. You go into it so open-heartedly. And then one review can potentially slam the door on everything that everybody felt. It's a lot of power that critics have. Their honesty holds a lot of power.

Do you feel like you must work hard to preserve your own artistic ambition? Is there a risk it becomes a smaller and smaller part of you when you're the artistic director of the companies you've run, and you're doing all the things those jobs involve?

It depends on the type of companies I have run. At Paines Plough, I directed everything. That's the way it was set up at the time, whereas now it is different. Then, at the National Theatre of Scotland, the focus was very much on what the company needed and not about me as a director, although I did direct some things there. The Royal Court sits somewhere between the two because the Royal Court has always been run by someone who also directs quite a lot of work, which is a glorious thing. So it's about creating a balance. The world, over the past few years, has been undergoing some brilliant changes and the questions being rightly asked about who has the right to occupy a space mean that I am less suitable and less able to direct everything that we programme at the Court. And that's a brilliant achievement, because although the things I can ally myself with feel very precious and hard won, the focus is not just on me as a director, which is great because the Royal Court would be terrible if we only programmed things that I would be suitable to direct.

I think in general that we're on the cusp of some big changes. I'm really interested in seeing what happens over the next five years or so, because I think there's going to be a significant shift in the model of how a theatre or a company is run. I don't know what the result will look like, but I think an important part of the puzzle will be the new generation of people who are happy to take leadership roles but don't need to be pushing themselves out at the front. I find it all very exciting. It feels like a transitional moment, and I think it will all lead to something great happening.

Yes, it feels like a moment where there is a lot of negativity or depressing things happening, but also real moments of positivity, hope and an appetite for change.

It's a disruption. We're at a point of huge disruption and that can always feel incredibly painful in some ways. It can be negative for so many reasons but, ultimately, we need disruption in order to renew and change. We will weather the disruption knowing there is something better ahead of us.

Natalie Ibu

Deep listening, scaling-up work and doing a vibe-check on actors

Natalie Ibu is the Artistic Director and joint Chief Executive of Northern Stage in Newcastle upon Tyne. Before taking this position, the Scottish director was the Artistic Director at tiata fahodzi, the groundbreaking British-African heritage contemporary theatre company. When first joining Northern Stage in 2020, she made it her mission to connect with local creatives by initiating a marathon series of one-to-one Zoom calls that anyone was welcome to join. As a director, her work for the theatre includes *Road* (2021), *The White Card* (2022) and *Protest* (2023).

'I've fallen back in love with the practice.'

We're talking at a time when you're just over a year into the job as Artistic Director of Northern Stage in Newcastle. Has the role and the experience turned out to be different than you expected?

Well, I've just directed my 'dream play': *Road* by Jim Cartwright, which I first read at university when I was twenty. It's a real privilege to have started my dream job with a dream play and now I get to dream up another project that feels just beyond my reach in the same way that *Road* felt out of my grasp at the start of my career. In terms of the job in general, I feel like I've built up a certain resilience. I wouldn't say the role fits me yet, but I'm starting to wear in the elbows and that feels good.

It is, however, very different to how I imagined it would be. One assumes that working at a larger organisation with more resources and more staff equals more capacity, but I feel like I've got less capacity! In my previous role leading the company tiata fahodzi, I had a core team of three, whereas now I have a team of thirty-six, and with that growth and scale comes a new set of challenges. For example, line management is very different in a large organisation, and while I always knew I could be a good and inspirational leader, being a good line manager is a different skill. In fact, to be a good line manager, you need presence, availability and capacity, and those are the same things that can get robbed from a person while they are busy being a leader. With that, and everything else, the focus has been on navigation and negotiation. But really, there's been so much going on and so much has been surprising, I wouldn't know where to start to describe it all.

When you started, you inaugurated the *So Good to Zoom You* project, which involved doing one Zoom call every day for a year with a different artist or creative from the North-East, as a way of getting to know the area and its artistic environment. How has that project gone and what themes or issues emerged from those conversations?

My first year at Northern Stage has been an exercise in deep listening, and *So Good to Zoom You* has been one part of that. We also put on round-tables where we invited artists from all different disciplines to come and talk to us about transformative moments in their careers, and what they felt they needed to support them. We also partnered with Improbable to host the open forum *Devoted and Disgruntled* here. The whole package has been about getting an idea of what this region is like, how it sees itself and what it needs.

A lot of the focus was on the characteristics of the North-East – I'd ask people things like, 'If the North-East was a person, what kind of person would they be?' – and about pinpointing what stories the area wants to tell about itself. A lot of the stories of the region focus on shipbuilding or coal mining, and they remain very male, very white, and very heteronormative, even though the area itself has changed. Which presents the opportunity of reimagining old stories for today and growing, crafting and nurturing new narratives about the people and the place.

There was also a very specific, practical challenge that I came across. One of the things that I think is specific to the area and our theatre is the journey of scale for artists making work for our stages. At Northern Stage, our main space – Stage One – is technically a midscale stage. Whilst I have previous midscale experience, when I directed *Road* for that space, I realised that it's not like other midscale spaces. The auditorium might be midscale, but the stage is beyond. It is big and wide – it can be intimidating.

What became clear from all our conversations was that the North-East has this really rich cultural and theatrical scene, and artists are passionate about having the opportunity to make work in their home theatre, so the question then becomes about how we can support an

IBU

artist's journey and development towards making work for a space like Stage One.

Could you say a little more about the physical characteristics of Stage One that make it a particularly challenging space to create work for?

Yes, it's really wide! Like almost sixteen feet wide, which is extraordinarily wide. When we're in co-production and the work is touring to other midscale venues after us, the set designers must come up with a design that works here, but also enables us to basically leave half of it at home and only take the middle bit on tour. There's so much about the space that's amazing and exhilarating to work and perform in. It's unlike any other stage in England and, in many ways, feels like this wonderful playground for directors and designers. I had the luxury of rehearsing *Road* on Stage One for several weeks, which helped me to get to know the space and understand what it demands. And part of that was learning its challenges. *Road*, for example, is a play that requires a courageous vision and a boldness. It has a punk swagger all of its own and it doesn't play by the rules. But even with a play like that, there were moments that got lost on Stage One. For instance, there was this highly emotional monologue performed by a young female character whose husband is unemployed and, as a result, is lost, doesn't fit into the family home, drinks, and is abusive. And we created this amazing scene where the actress gave the most startling, vulnerable performance. Yet as soon as we were on Stage One, we couldn't see her eyes or her expressions. Stage One swallowed the scene.

Overcoming things like that is really tough, and I wouldn't have understood how to approach them until I had the experience of working in that specific space. Which crystallises the conundrum: How do you invite artists to think, imagine and make work at this scale if they haven't worked at this scale before?

In a related way, were issues of changing scale something that came up when you made or programmed work for tiata fahodzi? I mean,

if you're making work for a touring company that's going to all these different-sized venues and theatres, does that lead to very particular problems for a director?

Yes, very much so. It was very challenging. Partly because my vision for tiata fahodzi was about multiplying the narrative about what it means to be of African heritage and living in Britain. And part of multiplying the narrative was a question of scale. We felt that work led by Black artists was so often contained by or restricted by studio scale, and that was partly because of white supremacy that says that work is niche and can only speak to a very small amount of people, and partly because of the racism that says our work needs to be hyper-naturalistic and, therefore, you need to be close to it to engage with that naturalism and realism.

We programmed and produced *good dog* by Arinzé Kene, a show that was two-and-a-half-hour-long monologue that followed a young boy growing up on an estate over ten years, where he suffered from a kind of neglect of attention, so he was sort of invisible to everyone in his life. But that same invisibility afforded him this incredible privilege of access where he could see everything, and he knew everyone's secrets. We imagined and planned that show to be midscale because it felt like this 'state of the nation' play about community and multicultural cities, and about being othered from the world and about being lost. But despite creating this show for the midscale, in order to give it the far-reaching tour it deserved, we had to compromise, and it had to be squashed into some studio spaces.

The real cost of making it smaller was that the show lost its artistic gesture and so much else. It was designed to have a set that was a 3x3x3-metre cube – in some lights an impressionistic tower block, in others an expressionistic 'elephant in the room' – that the boy sort of uses as a climbing frame. He moves around it, he goes on top of it, it sets on fire, it's just this incredible piece of art by designer Amelia Jane Hankin. But the institutionally problematic views which confined it to a small scale suffocated the work, they did to the work what the play talks about the government doing to Black, brown and working-class communities. All of which shows how hard it can be to balance the artistic gesture with the realities of being a touring company and relying on the theatres that book you to really get behind the work – both artistically but also politically.

Which also, in a way, links to why I wanted to work in a building: because I wanted the opportunity to go on a long-term journey with audiences. When you're in a touring company you're just a guest, going into someone's house to meet their friends. You don't have an audience, you borrow an audience and you rely on the existing relationship that building has with its audience. When you're a Black-led theatre company, making work in a context that has historically marginalised and excluded the communities you're making work for, that's a really difficult situation. The audience you're making the work for often aren't at those theatres. Often you only go to a venue once and then never return, which means there's no opportunity to be in dialogue with the place or the people who come to that place to watch theatre. I see being an artistic director of a building as being a lot about that brokering and hosting, which requires consistency and deeply getting to know a place and its people.

In terms of balancing the practical considerations of being an artistic director – such as programming choices or booking tours – with the artistic gesture of a work, do you think it is harder to find a balance between all the administrative sides of AD work and your own commitments as an artist at a big organisation like Northern Stage than a smaller one like tiata fahodzi?

It's difficult to answer that because I really at TF – balancing the Chief Exec and management part of the job with the artistic bit. I think the thing that has significantly changed for me over the past year is that, up until recently, I always saw myself as a creative producer-type artistic director who didn't need to always be the one who was in the room making the work. That wasn't what was motivating me to be an artistic director. Which is an unusual perspective to have, as – historically – artistic directors start off as directors and only move into artistic leadership after doing a lot of their own artistic work.

At the time, the idea that I might be more concerned with audience development, the bar café offer and the diversity of the workforce than the plays, was hard for boards to understand sometimes, because they often wanted me to talk more about the productions we would be creating. But something changed when I directed *Road* this past year. Due to the coronavirus pandemic, it was the first time I'd been in a rehearsal room for ten months. Suddenly having the opportunity to direct a company of scale, with ten actors in it, made me realise that, 'Oh gosh, I need this to be part of my leadership practice.' I need time to be making my own work and, what's more, it is here in this rehearsal room that I feel like I've come home. This is where things feel instinctive, where change feels possible, where I feel like I can genuinely 'do' the job and 'understand' the job. Everything else about being an artistic director in a post-pandemic world feels impossible, but making plays I can do.

I realised, ultimately, that I need to feel close to the art and close to a room full of actors in order to have the energy and the confidence to do all the other stuff. That's something I wouldn't have said when I was at TF, and something I don't think I would even have understood until recently, when I went back into rehearsals.

In so many ways that sounds like a really exciting place to be...

I've fallen back in love with the practice, I guess. Previously, I was a bit judgy about those artistic directors who directed loads of their own season and were always in the rehearsal room. I thought that seemed selfish and limited the opportunities for other creatives. But now I realise there is something very replenishing and very essential about being in that space.

Let's talk a little about that space. Are there certain practices or activities or routines that you return to as part of creating that energising, replenishing rehearsal room?

It depends on the play and the people. Generally, particular practices and routines come out when I'm trying to get us all out of the head and into the body, when I'm trying to turn what is essentially an intellectual exercise into one that has been lived. I do a lot of physicalising, which focuses on getting a section of dialogue – for example, one particular line – out of the head and into the body. And then, eventually, back into the head. I also find music a particularly effective way of engaging with actors and with the text, and sometimes accessing a particular feeling in a different way. That can be particularly useful if I feel like everyone has hit a sort of block and I need to unlock something, but my notes aren't getting us where we need to go. There was one incredible moment in the rehearsals for *Road* where the four actors who end the play were listening to Otis Redding. We were in week three or four, so pretty far into rehearsals, and I asked them to come out of the set and stand in a circle and make eye contact with each other while listening to the song. And everyone – everyone – was in tears. And we were all in tears, just watching them.

I'm not proclaiming to be a magician or to have the magic key to unlocking something, but it's all about finding ways of reminding ourselves of what the heart of the thing we're making is. Because sometimes, after you've gone on this long journey of enquiry and delved into all these layers, and practised it so many times, it can be easy to forget the raw question or raw emotion that started the whole process.

And how do you discover the artists and actors that are going to be best suited to going on that journey into the play with you? For example, do you have a particular method or theory you use when auditioning people?

I love talking about auditioning because I think it is one of the most misunderstood processes. Every director goes into an audition hoping that the actor is the one they're looking for, and the actor hopes they're the one too. For me, it is about getting a certain vibe or feeling from a person. I can tell very quickly if someone is a 'good' actor or not – whatever 'good' really means. But the majority of the process – the recalls and any meetings I have with an actor – are really about answering the question of whether we are going to enjoy each other's company. As in: Are we going to get along? Because, for five to six weeks, I am going to see you more often than I see anyone else. Which means you will be there when I am on my period and when I haven't had breaks, and when I am hungry and when I am angry. And I need to know that we're going to be okay together and you're going to be an okay person to be around.

The first round of auditions is essentially meeting people to see who is interesting and who is a good actor. The second round is where I will give notes – and I'll give those even if you've done a perfect reading of something. I'll give the notes mainly to see what your attitude to receiving notes is, and also what your attitude is to things like play, uncertainty, risk and vulnerability. I have a casting director who says she can tell when I like an actor because I end up just rehearsing them. I really take my time getting to know them, and often that includes giving them a lot of notes, not because they necessarily need the notes but because I'm interested in working with them.

In many ways, I see the whole audition process as sort of like a series of dates. I think I'm ultimately looking to make sure we feel safe with each other. Which isn't to say that difficult conversations won't take place or people won't get upset – although I hope that in my rehearsal rooms that is a rarity – but that we basically feel good about being around each other and I feel like you're a person to trust.

I learnt early on in my career to trust my instincts. On the occasions when I've ignored a gut feeling about an actor, that initial 'thing' I felt worried about has always come back to haunt me. Like, if someone has an inability to take notes or listen fully to me, that was often pre-empted by, for example, an initial reticence to make eye contact. Ultimately, I'm looking for sense of chemistry from them. Your first take on a character doesn't need to be perfect – that's why I'm here, and we can work on that together later – but it's the 'how you work' that's really of interest to me.

Milli Bhatia

Politics and playwriting

Milli Bhatia is a dramaturg, and director of theatre, film and radio. She started out as the trainee director, then Literary Associate at London's Royal Court Theatre, before being made an associate director there. Her hugely popular world-premiere production of Jasmine Lee-Jones's *seven methods of killing kylie jenner* (Royal Court, 2019 and 2021) was nominated for an Olivier Award and then toured internationally. She has directed productions at theatres including the Young Vic; the Royal Court; the Public Theater, NY; Woolly Mammoth, DC; Riksteatern; Dramaten; Bush Theatre; the Southbank Centre and Edinburgh International Festival. She is a former member of the prestigious Old Vic 12 programme, the National Theatre directors' programme, and a former associate artist at the Bush Theatre.

'I recognise the power of theatre to effect social change.'

Before becoming an associate director at the Royal Court, you worked at the same theatre as a literary associate while also directing shows. It feels increasingly common for directors to have multiple other job roles, so I wanted to start by talking to you about your work within the building's literary department. What did your job there involve, and how did it link to your work as a director and dramaturg?

I've had the unique experience of exploring three different roles at the Royal Court. When I was a literary associate, I worked as part of a team of four which included the brilliant Literary Manager, Jane Fallowfield. My responsibilities included supporting the writers under commission at various stages of development, including during rehearsals and previews, and fostering new relationships. It also involved reading lots and lots of plays; writing to and meeting with writers and offering them dramaturgical support and feedback; contributing to artistic planning and script meetings; managing the script submissions and pool of readers and supporting the writer-led playwriting groups the Royal Court facilitates each year. A lot of that work is dramaturgical in nature.

It was an education in working with writers, and I've taken so much of my experience in the department into my practice as a director. The main difference to my work as a freelance director is that when working within the department, I'd consider the artistic mission of the organisation. But overall, I was just really able to hone my existing skillset. Along with working as a dramaturg, I've primarily directed new work, and there has always been a process of dramaturgy when doing that. Each piece of work has been different, but sometimes during the process of development leading up to rehearsals I've worked with a writer from early – or even first – drafts. And on other occasions similar work has largely taken place during rehearsals.

There is no single way of working with a writer, nor of supporting the development of a play. It's due to my experience at the Royal Court that I've become adept at listening to a play, which now feeds into the way I direct and the questions I'll ask of the play, whether I'm approaching it with a production in mind or supporting the writer in development. It has also furthered my understanding of how the development of each individual play needs to be bespoke. Each time I work on a new play, the process is different.

When you mention asking certain questions of any play you're working on, what exactly are those questions?

It depends on the stage of the process, but my approach essentially comes down to listening to the play. Crucially, as a director and dramaturg of new work, I don't wish to impose a vision onto a play or to steer the writer towards the play I think it should be or indeed the play I would most like to direct, but to ask questions that either help me in understanding what the most useful route of development might look like, or in better understanding the writer's vision in order to craft my own. I want to interrogate each decision the writer has made. I begin by searching for the answers in the text and if they aren't to be found, I look to the writer. Understanding the writer's intention will guide me to the execution of ideas and the nature of the process we embark on. I see my responsibility as supporting a writer in unearthing the play that they want to write, and asking the questions that will enable the play and production to flourish.

I know the feeling of reading a new draft without an initial clear instinct of how to stage it far too well – because I'm excited by ambitious plays and writers that throw down the theatrical gauntlet. This is why a forensic eye is useful; I'm hunting for the clue that will unlock something. Jasmine Lee-Jones once spoke about the characters in *seven methods of killing kylie jenner* as 'glitching', which appears once in the text, in a direction that prefaces the play. This one reference became the foundation for how myself, designer Rajha Shakiry, movement director Delphine Gaborit, lighting designer Jessica Hung Han Yun and sound designer Elena Peña crafted two worlds and two languages that could crash together as they meet and then coalesce in the play.

Does the experience of working as a literary associate influence how you now read the plays that are sent to you as a director? Specifically, do you think it makes you more likely, or able, to see the potential in a script even if it's messy and unfinished? Or, when you're reading a script 'as a director' are you only interested in plays that feel like the finished article?

As a director, I can be thrilled by a play even if it's in its early stages of development. I first read *seven methods of killing kylie jenner* when it was a ten-page lyrical poem and would have directed it even if Jasmine Lee-Jones hadn't expressed an ambition to develop it further. Collaboration is the key here: I don't ever expect to pick up a play and see the entirely finished article when it is written by a living writer, because so much discovery happens in rehearsal. In the process on each new play, I've worked with the writer by my side at every stage. The play we go into rehearsals with is rarely exactly what is put in front of an audience. As long as I am fundamentally excited by the possibility of the play in front of me, I'm all in. The intrusive 'How the fuck do I stage this?' thought that might creep in after a very first read is thrilling. It's a provocation to dig deeper into the text. As a director of new work, you must hold your nerve and put your trust in the process you will go into. There are no guarantees or absolutes.

I remember reading *seven methods of killing kylie jenner*, which you first directed at the Royal Court in 2019, and being so excited by how it physically appears on the page, with all the embedded emojis and gifs. Not many playwrights write plays that are as interesting to read as they are to see performed. What produces that shot of excitement in you which causes you to think: I need to be the one to direct this play?

I'm interested in theatrical scope, form, and how the writer considers audience but, crucially, I'm most interested in the writer's voice. This is true of many plays I've directed; I also had the feeling you describe when first reading *Baghdaddy* by Jasmine Naziha Jones, *Chasing Hares* by Sonali Bhattacharyya, and *Blue Mist* by Mohamed-Zain Dada. On reflection, I've found that what connects a lot of the work I've made are the themes of power, identity and grief. They have all awakened something in me and, fundamentally, I read them and believed in their power and necessity. It's such a privilege to be trusted with a new play, and I've been lucky to direct several writers' very first plays. It does feel a little like being handed a baby and being told, 'It's ours now and I'm trusting you not to drop it.'

You've mentioned what could be called the politics of a play a few times. Could you talk a little more about what that phrase means to you?

I've talked about my interest in how a writer considers audience, as I recognise the power of theatre to effect social change. I don't necessarily mean staging a dialectical discussion of a political issue, I'm interested in artists who consider how their politics intersect with form and who they choose to tell stories about; and who understand that the act of theatre-making, a communal imaginative space and an invitation to another perspective all have the ability to change us. Theatre enlists imagination and can invite us not just to look at our reality, but to search for alternatives.

Much of my political education has come from reading plays and watching theatre. Watching Yaël Farber's *Nirbhaya* as a student inspired me to volunteer for a South Asian women's refuge and dig deeper on my own educational journey into Indian feminism and women's rights. I also became more directly involved in political organising and protest at this time, so much of which is theatre.

I approach the process of directing a play by asking similar questions to those one might when organising political action, and I came to both directing and political organising around the same time, in my late teens. 'Why this and why now?'; 'Who is it for?'; 'Who is the audience?'; 'How do we consider spectacle and theatricality?'; 'Who will it speak to?' and 'Who do we want to empower within the process of creating and staging this event?' are some examples. I consider how I can be clear and precise about what my work wants to do, and how I can practise resistance, responsibility and solidarity in the process. Drawing on the way some activists organise direct action has helped me be clearer about that. I've worked with many artists that consider their art a vehicle for their politics.

Does the politics of a work also inform the 'behind the scenes' part of creating a show?

Absolutely. For instance, *seven methods* was created with a cast and creative team made up entirely of women. For the conversations we needed to be having to be effective, they needed to take place between women.

Moving on to a slightly different subject, I noticed that you worked quite extensively as an assistant director before moving on to directing your own work. What was your experience of being an assistant like and what did you take from being one?

I assisted many inspiring directors, including some whose practice and tastes couldn't be further from my own. But, in general, being an assistant is one of the most valuable things I did because it's an opportunity to observe someone else's process which, as a director now, I never get to do. You are able to absorb all the wins while also witnessing the decisions that don't quite land, which is just as valuable.

I experienced the joy of being a sponge in rehearsal rooms where new plays were being made, and it was from assisting that I learnt what kind of rehearsal room and working environment I wanted to facilitate. But there comes a point when you just have to put your philosophies, theories and learning into practice.

I had a fairly unique experience because the transition between assisting and directing happened very suddenly for me. In 2019, I was an assistant director on a play at the Royal Court and then, later that same year, I was directing in the very same space. That was all down to Vicky Featherstone, the former Artistic Director at the Royal Court, who has consistently supported and championed me.

Along with all the positive things about being an assistant director, was there anything you found frustrating or not so great about it?

It can be frustrating when, as an assistant, you're sitting on the edge of your seat bursting with offers and ideas, but without an opportune moment to share them with the director. However, I was fortunate with the directors I assisted as most of them were open to my input and trusting of my voice in the room.

I experienced some imposter syndrome early in my career, some of which was due to the way I was spoken to or perceived in certain spaces, and what many of the directors around me looked like. This is sometimes still the case, it just becomes easier to navigate when you refuse to shrink yourself in order to accommodate others. Much of that confidence came due to the support of directors and leaders that I worked alongside.

Was there a particular point when you noticed that your confidence had significantly grown?

It was all part of a process that involved witnessing these incredible artists of the global majority – leaders, facilitators and directors – who were creating the kind of environments I wanted to be in. In my early twenties, I worked at the Bush Theatre and Madani Younis, the former Artistic Director, and the Associate Director Omar Elerian were very supportive. It was Madani that gave me my first ever professional production. I was so excited by how they worked with other artists and encouraged a process of collaboration. It was a similar story with the directors I assisted such as Pooja Ghai, Roxana Silbert and Lynette Linton, plus Simeilia Hodge-Dallaway, who created Artistic Directors of the Future, a programme for directors of the global majority who aspired to become artistic directors. The programme included events where we would meet existing artistic directors, which is how I first met Vicky Featherstone.

It's vital that I recognise the support and access that I have been given by other artists, and pay that forward. The community of artists around me has been an important part of my successes.

Jamie Fletcher

Making music
and finding a home in theatre

Jamie Fletcher is a director and musician. She is a northern, neurodivergent, working-class, queer and trans woman; her background and identity informs the work that she makes. Initially starting her career performing and making music, live art, cabaret and devised performances, she now specialises in creating and directing musical theatre, multidisciplinary performance, comedy and work with socio-political themes. The driving force behind all her work is a deep commitment to sharing queer and trans stories and telling existing stories through a queer and trans lens. Jamie's directing highlights include the critically acclaimed UK revival of *Hedwig and the Angry Inch*, co-produced by Leeds Playhouse and HOME Manchester (2022) and the Fringe First Award-winning *Happy Meal* by Tabby Lamb, co-produced by Roots and Theatre Royal Plymouth (2022–23).

'I felt that the world of "theatre" wasn't for someone like me.'

A lot of your work for theatre involves a significant amount of music. How did you come to make this kind of work and what role does music play for you?

Music has always been a really big part of my life – and, in many ways, the underscore to it as well. Music is something we attach so much emotion to, especially when we are young, and there are always songs that can immediately take us back to a particular place or experience. Growing up, I was always compelled to play and write music. I come from a working-class family and we didn't really go to the theatre. But when I was ten, I got the opportunity to see *The Phantom of the Opera* at the Palace Theatre in Manchester, and I was really blown away by the spectacle of it all, the live music and the magic of theatre. It was really special, as a kid, to see something like that. I knew then that I wanted to do that.

Anyway, music and theatre remained my big interests but when I reached high school, I wasn't allowed to take both Music and Drama – although I did keep performing the lead roles in school shows as an extra-curricular thing. I hated school, I couldn't understand why I wasn't allowed to study more creative subjects that I was clearly good at and passionate about. After finishing my GCSEs, I went on to what was then Leeds College of Music – it's since been fancily rebranded as Leeds Conservatoire! – and I studied Popular Music, Performance and Composition. During my final year, the college started offering a Musical Theatre BTEC National Diploma, and even though I couldn't gain that qualification, I asked to go to all the classes as an extra. I just loved musical theatre and wanted to learn. I didn't think I could pursue theatre without qualifications, but on my UCAS form I put down a wildcard and applied to do a BA joint honours in Music and Drama degree at Manchester Met. I'm so thankful I did as it worked out. In my second year, I was selected for the director's pathway on the course and began directing plays, making contemporary theatre and exploring how music and performance went together. It was also while I was at university that I met Divina De Campo. We had lots of shared interests and formed a band together, and Divina has become a long-term collaborator of mine. Gradually, the two threads of music and drama naturally fused. I would often compose music for the shows I was making or collaborate with other musicians. I like utilising live music as part of a storytelling device and incorporating sound design to help bring out different aspects of a show, whether that's creating an atmosphere, heightening an emotion, giving a hint of nostalgia or something else entirely. Music does so much for a story; you wouldn't dream of watching a film and turning off the musical underscore.

After university, I couldn't afford to continue studying or training, and opportunities felt scarce and hard to come by. It felt like the world of 'theatre' wasn't for someone like me. However, I was lucky enough for my final-year university shows to be picked up by Battersea Arts Centre and Greenroom and hÅb arts Manchester, where I became a commissioned artist. So I gravitated more towards the live-art and cabaret scene and making work of that kind, although I did do a big TIE (theatre-in-education) tour, which was an experience. At the time, it felt like the live-art scene was perhaps a bit more progressive and accepting of 'weirdos' and being queer, and it felt important to find other people who were like me and welcomed me. I went on to collaborate with a range of artists and companies and make all sorts of different kinds of performance work, like one piece in 2009 that involved pushing a fourteen-and-a-half-foot boat 105 miles around Yorkshire and stopping off at places to perform a song or do a little performance, and also asking people to write their values onto this giant boat. It was while I was making this kind of work that I realised what actually matters most to me is the audience and the story. The audience is the real reason I make anything. Gradually, I started working more with writers and exploring that relationship between playwright and director. I began moving towards making new work and musical-theatre shows in a more traditional touring theatre setting, and then directing plays and musicals on a bigger scale.

Art is my activism. That's why I am passionate about sharing queer and trans stories on the big stage. I'm also conscious that we all want bums on seats, and audiences want to have a good time. The accessibility and wide appeal of music helps me to tell big, beautiful, universal stories which can reach a diverse audience and open up new perspectives.

Does your training in music and experience being a musician come in useful now you're working as a director?

Yes. I like to work really closely with the musical director, sound designer and musicians. Having a musical background means we are all, literally, speaking the same language. Which means we can all get to the same place quicker. I think sometimes when musicians are working on a production, a director can say something to them about the music, using terms that each person understands differently. For example, a director without any musical experience might refer to one part of the show as that bit where the music speeds up – when it actually doesn't, it's that the instrumentation is now playing staccato semiquaver rhythms! When I was directing *Hedwig and the Angry Inch*, I was able to talk about the details of the song arrangements and the exact guitar or drum sounds I wanted, and then Alex Beetschen (the musical director) and I could geek out together and have a shared vision.

There's also the non-verbal communication that you get when you're collaborating with other musicians. You don't always have to say something out loud, there's just this feeling when something is working or not working. And when we do need to verbally communicate, then there's all that shared technical language which allows for so much more nuance.

You mentioned feeling that theatre wasn't 'for someone like you'. What changed to make you feel like you could work in this world?

It took a long time for me to feel at home in theatre. I think it's all to do with how a community, or an industry, creates spaces that allow you to feel welcomed, and opens doors for you. It's something I hope I can continue to do for other people because that's the culture shift we desperately need. For too long, it's been straight, cisgender, middle-class, white men who have dominated the industry. When these people are in – for want of a better term – gatekeeping positions or positions of power, and they think that inviting other groups in to tell their stories is a producing and programming 'risk', or think there isn't an audience for 'this kind of work', then we have a problem. We need to diversify our audiences. We need to not only invite artists in, but to give them real opportunities to train, to advance and to tell their own stories.

There are currently not many trans women directors working at the mid–large scale. There are still barriers to the industry for so many people. Often they are not given paid opportunities, or aren't given the support to develop their skills at a larger scale. When working on *Hedwig*, for example, a big part of my focus was on getting the theatre and the producers on board with a certain vision. It was about the importance of diversifying the room and working hard to help make people feel truly welcome and supported, allowing them to flourish so they can do the best job they can. That's something that's not always done, partly because in theatre, time and money are usually working against you. So what often happens, in reality, is that you go, 'Okay, I'm going to diversify my room, where can I find some trans projection designers?' And then, once you've actually found some, you then ask how many of them have had experience working at this particular scale. The fact is that very few have, because almost none have been given the opportunities or granted that extra bit of training that allows them to feel confident and, in turn, allows the producers bankrolling the project to feel confident. So, with *Hedwig*, it was important for us to give people the opportunities and the extra support where we could.

What did that 'extra support' look like in practice?

So, I had an assistant director working with me, but I also had a trainee assistant director as well. We also had people come in at different times to be there to just observe, learn and gain an insight, without the pressure and responsibility of a particular job to do. Our lighting designer also had an associate who was learning alongside them. We were unable to secure a trans projection designer with the experience and availability for this project, so instead we brought on board a talented and experienced cisgender projection designer who then animated illustrations by a trans artist. Our aim was to make things more authentic and diversify the voices present and, in order to do that, we needed to find slightly different ways to work. Another factor to consider was around the importance of casting trans performers who, again, might not yet have had the opportunity to be on those big stages, and offering them the right guidance, support and encouragement to be able to do that. Because I knew they were amazing and, with the right support, the results were astounding.

We also made sure training was in place for other members of staff working in the theatres. We needed to ensure everyone understood that we were bringing in a creative team and company of trans and queer people, including actors, musicians, designers and stage managers, and so we needed to work together to make sure it was a welcoming, supportive and affirmative environment. Actually, more than affirmative. We needed it to be a celebratory atmosphere, so people could flourish as themselves and bring their best self to the work.

And, finally, we put in place therapy sessions for trans members of the company if they wanted it. When you've got trans creatives involved and performers on stage telling a trans story that deals with trauma, they're bringing themselves to the show and some of the work might trigger things for them. We wanted to provide an outlet for them to speak to someone if they needed to. It's all about their wellbeing – if you're doing a show eight times a week or whatever, you've got to feel okay about what you are doing, and you've got to be able to walk away from the material when you need to. It's difficult and it doesn't always happen in the industry, but creating a safe space for artists is so important to me.

Before we spoke, you also mentioned in an email how important creating safe spaces was to you and your work. When you said that,

were you referring to the rehearsal space, like you just mentioned, or did you also mean the theatre space in general?

Both. It's also about the theatre itself and the audiences. When creating a piece of theatre, you have to think about the audience and what their reactions might be to things. I would never just pick up a play and assume that everything in it would be fine for an audience in 2023, or whenever, to watch. Racism, queerphobia, ableism, fatism and misogyny are rife in many pre-existing plays and musicals, so adjustments often need to be made. It's about weaving things in and out to create something that feels right and is appropriate and true for an audience right now.

And it's about more than just what's on stage. I'm particularly proud of the relationship I've developed with Leeds Playhouse over the years. When I directed *Dancing Bear* there in 2016 and 2018, we did trans training with all of the staff and we encouraged the theatre to change all the toilet signage so that all our audience members would feel welcome. Since then, things have changed much more widely across the industry, so it should no longer be the responsibility of a visiting company to address things like that. It has to now be the venue making those choices and getting on board with things. Since around the time of the pandemic, we've been in a different place. There's a lot more knowledge and awareness out there, and lots of places are doing things to make artists and audiences feel more welcome.

I'm in a fortunate position. The director is usually the person that gets to choose the creative team and be involved in the casting decisions. So, I feel very lucky to be meeting lots of amazing people and getting to collaborate with them. I like, above all, to lead by example and I wear my heart on my sleeve. By being open about my identity and the things I find difficult, I can create a space where other people can be open and are able to check in with each other. I bring my core values, my activism and my politics into every rehearsal room and, even when a process is short, I think we should all prioritise doing that. Ultimately, we're making art and that's a real privilege. It's a beautiful thing, so it shouldn't be a horrible experience! We should be able to be kind to each other and still make something special. It's up to me as the director to help to create an environment where everyone can thrive and have a good time. An audience can tell when a show has been made with honesty, authenticity, love and kindness. It kind of seeps into the show itself and, in the end, creates a better piece of work.

You mentioned that you took a slightly non-traditional route into being a director. I think sometimes people can feel insecure about taking a different route into the industry, so I wondered if you thought there were any positives to your own experience?

Very much so. I mean, paid development opportunities and funding is always an issue and has been a major hurdle for me across my career. I couldn't afford to do an MA and I didn't do those kind of internships and directing schemes where you needed to suddenly be available for three months or more, because I needed to earn a more stable income – which is something a lot of freelance directors and artists need to do. We often have to become entrepreneurial with earning money through lecturing or teaching or running workshops or whatever it might be. I taught regular peripatetic music lessons at a school and led a ton of workshops with different organisations too. I also directed a lot of youth-theatre and community productions, all of which definitely helped me hone some of my directing and leadership skills further, particularly about how to run a room and work with a big group of people, as well as how to get the best out of someone quickly and efficiently. I think it's more common than people realise for directors to do what I did, which is to carve their own path and take a slightly different route in, partly through necessity.

Above all, I think the thing my experience taught me was about different kinds of audiences and how people connect with what we put on stage. I also learnt a lot about the environment we create around a show and, through collaboration with a range of artists, creatives and organisations, different approaches to making theatre. That's how I came to making what might be called 'multidisciplinary theatre'. I'm constantly learning and drawing on all these different styles, methods and techniques that I've learnt and explored, and that interest me. I don't ever want to limit myself by saying, 'This is the box that I'm working in.' Bringing in different disciplines and fusing things together makes for a real richness. I'm not a traditional kind of girl; I like to push things forward and find things that are new and fresh. That doesn't mean I would never tackle something historical or traditional, or that's part of the Western canon, but that if I did, the aim would be to place a new lens over it and understand why it's important to share this with an audience now.

One of the things I learnt through experience is that although I feel confident being the 'one in charge', I prefer to now work in a way that feels less hierarchical. I've found a way to direct that centres kindness, respect, trust, openness, vulnerability, communication and a clear vision. I've got to that place partly by working out what hasn't worked for me personally when creating theatre. As a northern, working-class, neurodivergent, queer, trans woman, I've had to figure out why certain spaces and environments haven't been the best for me to be in. That includes looking at the times when I have got things wrong and learning from those experiences so I can now create spaces other people are going to be empowered in. For me, collaboration is the key to making great theatre and so I always want to get the best out of the people I am working with. I believe we should all be able to find a way to get behind a shared vision and create incredible things together. It's a privilege and a joy to be able to do what we do – so it shouldn't be theatre purgatory!

Tamara Harvey

Motherhood and making it all work

In June 2023, Tamara Harvey became the Co-Artistic Director of the Royal Shakespeare Company, alongside Daniel Evans. Prior to this, she was the Artistic Director of Theatr Clwyd in North Wales from 2015. During her time in charge, the unique theatre became both a thriving community-arts hub and one of the most admired producing theatres outside of London. Her directing work there included the Olivier Award-winning *Home, I'm Darling* (2018), written by long-term collaborator Laura Wade. She is also an advocate for the rights of working parents in the theatre industry.

'I cling to the belief that it's a battle worth fighting.'

I wanted to talk to you about two broad topics: one, how you, as an artistic director and director, make theatre 'work' for other people (those seeing it and those living close by to it) and two, how you make theatre 'work' for you, as an artist who is also a mother of two children. Starting with the first of those topics, there's a lot of conversation happening in the industry around getting new audiences into theatres. When you started at Theatr Clwyd, was that question a big part of your thinking for your time in charge? Or were you more interested in keeping and responding to an existing audience?

No, I did feel it was important. When I started at Clwyd there was clearly a core existing audience, but I think it would be fair to say they were an ageing audience and they represented quite a narrow band of society. Theatr Clwyd is up on a hill and, not least because of how the bricks and mortar look, it was perceived by a lot of people in the local community as a kind of fortress that wasn't for them. I came in very much determined to fling the doors open as wide as possible and get as many people as possible not necessarily seeing shows, but feeling as though the building belonged to them. I have a passionate belief that theatre buildings should be – particularly in more rural areas – spaces for everyone, irrespective of their attitude to theatre. So, for example, for the first three years we had an ice rink in the winter, because one of the young women in the youth theatre said we should have an ice rink. And that felt like a good way of going, 'There's something for everyone!'

Similarly, we started saying 'yes' to everything, like baby massage classes, because we wanted everyone to feel they could use the whole building, not just the stage. We also made a concerted effort to broaden the programming, both in terms of our produced and presented work. We wanted to be a broad church. I like that phrase because I think at this moment in history, when fewer of us are going to church or any kind of religious worship, theatre buildings become more important as spaces for thought and debate and shared communion. For us, this included ramping up our family programming, and programming for children and young people. We also started producing contemporary playwrights more and a lot more musicals, like *Rent*. All of it was a very deliberate move to try to broaden our appeal.

When you say 'something for everyone', does that mean you were hoping that, across a season, there would be something to appeal to different people or that you were looking to programme shows that had a broad appeal in themselves?

No, it was more that sense of across the season there would be different things for different people. It felt important that we were still, for example, having Rambert come visit and keeping the classical music season and North Wales Jazz. The idea was, exactly as you say, that you should be able to open the brochure and find something for you. There might not be something every night or every week, but there will be something for you over the course of a season.

Theatr Clwyd is, as you say, a unique building in a striking location. You mentioned trying to stop it feeling like a 'fortress' to local people. Were your programming decisions, then, largely about appealing to the local community or were you also trying to get people to visit from much further afield?

It was both. There was a very real feeling of wanting the people of Mold to be able to walk up the hill, because when we looked at the box-office data we had quite a wide radius with more people actually coming from further afield and fewer people coming from the immediate towns of Mold, Buckley, Flint and so on. That didn't feel fair, as we wanted people locally to feel it was their theatre. However, we also cast our eyes further afield in two senses. Firstly, by thinking about what people would travel for – and this was where our focus on new writing came from, because if you produce something no one else has ever produced then that's going to create a certain amount of buzz. We also wanted to be a major part of the ecosystem of new writing in Wales and be a home for contemporary playwriting. Secondly, we wanted to look at co-producing so that if people didn't want to travel to us to see the work we were making, they would be able to see it elsewhere. And, although totally unplanned, that became especially true during the pandemic when we were creating digital work or streaming things that could be seen by people all over the world.

You've talked about programming choices and other activities, but what do you think is the biggest barrier or challenge to getting – and keeping – new people coming through the doors?

I don't think there's any one thing. That's part of what's difficult because quite often we feel like there should be a silver bullet. For example, if we create cheap tickets: they'll book; if we sort out the transport: they'll book; if we get the marketing right: they'll book. Whereas, actually, I think there are lots of different things that prevent people coming to a theatre. Price point is one of them. You must figure out what makes it affordable and that will be different for everyone. I don't think free tickets are necessarily the answer because I think there is something important about that transaction, however small the amount of money, and making sure audiences understand there is a cost to creating stuff and that it can't just happen without any level of support. There is also something special about letting people into the process. We did quite a lot of work around open rehearsals, and bringing people in, whether that's schools, dementia groups, or whoever, so that theatre becomes demystified. Which sounds odd, doesn't it? Because often we feel like the mystery is integral to theatre, but increasingly I have found people enjoy theatre more if they've been let into the process. And then I think there are basic things like making sure people realise it doesn't matter what clothes they're wearing, or making sure the doors are clearly labelled so you don't feel stupid when you're trying to get in the building. Really, though, there are as many different reasons people don't come to the theatre as there are people, so all you can do is keep trying different things. The harder thing is getting people to come back more than once. Often, we can be really good at getting people to come once but creating a sense of loyalty so they come for a second time is equally as difficult, if not more so.

During your time at Theatr Clwyd, did you have any grand plans for bringing in new audiences that fell flat and didn't actually achieve what you hoped?

Oh, yes – the ice rink! I thought it was a brilliant, brilliant thing, but the third year in particular we had to cancel so many days, ironically because of snow. The snow would fall on the roof of the tent that we had over it, making it unsafe, plus people couldn't travel to it. We realised it just didn't make financial sense; we were haemorrhaging money. I was gutted because I thought it was a great way of opening up the building and making people feel like they could come here even if they didn't love theatre. Another thing that's been interesting is that whenever I've programmed – the word that springs to mind is 'cynically', although it hasn't felt cynical because it's about creating work that people want to see – but whenever I've programmed purely with a view to bums-on-seats and having a popular title in the mix alongside more obscure things, the audience has come, but tickets haven't flown off the shelves. The pessimist in me thinks that's because audiences can smell cynicism but, if I'm more generous, I think it's also because audiences want the exciting and the new. With a play, they want to see something that's a bit more unusual. They don't necessarily want another production of, I don't know, *The Importance of Being Earnest*.

Let's turn now to talking about how you make theatre work for you. On your Twitter account and elsewhere, you've talked a lot about the realities of being a mother to young children and a theatre director. To start, what do you think the major, practical challenges are to combining those two roles?

There's a real danger that I'll get emotional answering this. You're catching me at a moment where, as I approach starting the job as co-Artistic Director at the Royal Shakespeare Company, the thing that keeps me awake at night is whether, by applying for and accepting that job, I'm going to destroy my relationship with my kids. To answer the question, though: the truth is, I could put a spin on it. And the spin would be that I'm a better artistic director because I am a mother, and I'm a better mother because I'm doing something that I find fulfilling and that I love. But the truth is that there aren't enough hours in the day. As an AD, I don't see as many shows, spend as many hours reading plays, returning emails, meeting artists, as I would if I didn't have kids. And, as a mother, I don't spend as much time with my kids as I would if I wasn't an artistic director. So, I think the brutal truth is that it doesn't work.

Day to day, I am trying to find the best version of it there can be, but I think we are living in a difficult moment in history, as women, where we've fought and to some extent won the right to have a career and have children. Yet none of us – men, women, non-binary, everyone included – have figured out what that actually means. And I think a lot of the men, even the really good ones, aren't willing to take on the roles that are necessary in order for women to be able to do that. So, most of my friends who are mums still do most of the emotional carrying for the family and a lot of the practical sorting out, like managing childcare and having a good relationship with the nanny or the childminder and doing the laundry, doing all the chores. The major challenge remains time. One of the most difficult bits about theatre is that it starts at 7:30 in the evening and that's bedtime. I hate missing bedtime. Additionally, if you're an AD – or if you're a freelancer in the industry – it's almost impossible to take holidays, even if you're encouraged to do so.

But the biggest challenge of all is managing the guilt in my own head. Which is sometimes around not working hard enough as an artistic director and sometimes around not being there enough as a mum. And sometimes it's about how I'm doing both jobs. For example, last night I had a Zoom meeting at 8 p.m. with a playwright. I'd made it 8 so that I could do bedtime first, but the kids were being pixies. And it was getting closer and closer to 8 o'clock. And I was getting more and more stressed because I knew I had to be on this call and so I was getting like, 'Please, can you *just* brush your teeth? I want to do stories and songs, so, please, let's just get into bed.' And then, of course, I felt guilty for being the stressy mum. So, really, I don't know what the answer is. But I cling to the belief that it's a battle worth fighting.

Have you found that your openness in talking about this subject has meant that other mothers in the theatre industry have started talking to you about it as well?

Yes, they have, which is one of the things I'm most proud about as a result of speaking up. Doing so was a very deliberate thing. I'm not public about my life and I had never particularly engaged with social media before doing so. I only had a Twitter account because I'd done a show where a producer told me I had to have one. The first tweet I sent about being a working mum was because I was so cross with a guy at a bus stop who made some comment about how my child's feet must be cold at a moment when I was feeling really buzzed. I was so proud of myself because I'd got the older child to the childminder and the younger one in a sling, we were at the bus stop and I was going to get to rehearsals on time… and then this bloke said, 'Oh, cold feet, poor kid.' As it happened, I had his socks in my pocket, but he gets hot feet so I hadn't put them on yet. Anyway, I was so furious that I tweeted something about it – and it got a response. And in that moment, I thought, 'Oh, I need to do being a mum publicly because I have a job and it's secure, no one's going to fire me.' Freelancers struggle to talk about it so I will do it instead, I will shout about it a lot. Although I stopped doing so during the first bit of the pandemic because it felt irrelevant and a bit petty and there were people with much bigger problems than I had.

But anyway, it was a deliberate decision to talk about it and connected to the sense of responsibility I have as an artistic director to try and make the world better for other working parents or those with caring responsibilities. I also know that a couple of times it's lost me a gig, even as an artistic director. For instance, there was a co-production that was on the table, and I was slated to direct it, but the co-producer actually said, 'I just think she's got too much on her plate.' And referred to the kids. So yeah, I think we've got a long way to go but it's important to keep having the conversation.

Do you get the impression things are changing across the industry in ways that make it slightly easier for people to juggle work and home commitments?

To an extent. We're having the conversation more and some theatres, like Theatr Clwyd, are doing things like putting lines in the budget to help people with childcare. As an AD, I've been encouraging directors to do the entire rehearsal schedule in advance so that people know when they're needed and can arrange their lives around that. Part of the problem is that every child at every age has different needs. Which means theatres can't come up with a one-size-fits-all solution. My own needs as a working parent are totally different now to what they were five years ago, or even six months ago. People will sometimes ask why we don't have a nursery or a crèche, and the answer is because the percentage of people coming to work for us who that would help is tiny, and the numbers wouldn't support the nursery being open. What's actually more important to that person is that we pay them enough so they're able to go home for a long weekend to spend time with their families. I think, slowly, the industry is changing, but these are knotty, difficult questions. The important thing will always be having the conversation.

For you, is the cliché of being more efficient because of having children, and therefore less time, true, or is it actually the case that less time simply equals more stress?

I think it's partially true. It varies person to person – I know a couple of writers for whom that's definitely true. They sit down and get work done, whereas they used to procrastinate for an hour before they wrote that scene. I wish it were truer for me, but I don't feel like I'm particularly more efficient than I was. It certainly means I get less sleep because I tend to do things while they're asleep, which means I work later. I miss the early mornings because before I had kids, if I had a deadline I knew that whatever happened, I could get up at 5 a.m. and get a couple of hours' work done before everyone else was awake. Now, I don't dare do that because the kids are bound to wake up when I do – it's like they have a sixth sense, a Spidey sense. Or I can't rely on it because they might have been up four times in the night and I'll be on my knees, and if I don't sleep from 5 to 7 I'll want to shoot myself. That's the bit I miss. To know whether I'm more efficient than I was before, you'd have to ask my colleagues.

We've talked about all the challenges but, despite those, what makes it all worth it in the end?

I just love it. And I think it's really important. Stories are how we figure out who we are and how to be alive. For me and for lots of people I know, live stories, theatre, does that more potently than anything else. When we get it right, whether it's the stories on our stages or the work in our communities, it can genuinely change lives. It can rescue people or make them see the world in a way that means they will change the world themselves. It gives people a reason to get up in the mornings, which is why I keep doing it. And because – some of the time, anyway – I truly believe it makes the world a better place.

Annabel Arden

The theatre of opera

Annabel Arden is an actor, deviser and prolific international director of theatre and opera. After training in Paris with Jacques Lecoq, Monika Pagneux and Philippe Gaulier, she co-founded the now-famous Complicité with Simon McBurney and Marcello Magni. After a decade of creating and performing in Complicité shows, she began also directing work independently. Her extensive list of credits includes plays at the Almeida, National Theatre and Royal Court. She has also directed opera in the USA and widely across Europe.

'It's a chemical process...'

You've worked extensively in theatre and in opera and, here, I wanted to talk to you mainly about your work in opera, but from the perspective of someone who crosses between both worlds. My first question is simply, is there something integrally different about directing opera to directing theatre?

It's the question you're always asked. They have felt different at different points in my career but, ultimately, no. With both, you have to tell a story and you have to transport an audience. If they're watching opera, they might have to suspend disbelief in a different way than perhaps they would in theatre, but you want them to be carried away by the story and the emotional realities of what they're seeing. In all forms of live performance, you want the audience and the performers to believe in whatever the stylistic realities of the work are, whether it's a Brechtian representation or more naturalistic. Opera lends itself to heightened reality and often requires stylisation.

However, the quintessential difference with opera is that the tempo is not created by the singers alone. The tempo is a shared thing between the singers, the orchestra and the conductor. That doesn't happen in theatre because there is no conductor and no orchestra. For the music to work on a technical level, the singers can't hugely vary the tempo. Of course, it used to be much more the case that if you were a great star like Maria Callas, you could do whatever the hell you wanted with the tempo, and it's still kind of true that the conductor has to breathe with and follow the individual singer. Yet, really, when you've got a large, orchestrated piece with a big chorus, there is only one tempo. So, if you think that aria would sound much better sung much slower, well, you have to negotiate that.

Cuts to the text are also more difficult, although conductors are becoming more open to that now. If you do a big Shakespeare as a theatre director, you will often be considering what to cut and what not to cut. It's much more difficult to do that with opera. Partly because, technically, it's not my job to cut the score. The score belongs to the conductor. Ideally, I forge a relationship with that person and we sit with the score together, and we could say, 'This was created in the eighteenth century for a completely different kind of spectacle, let's reorder it.' And people are becoming more open to that, but when I started twenty-five, thirty years ago, the music was a sacred cow and you couldn't touch any of it. All this means you don't have sole possession of the text in the way that a theatre director does, because you're not the one who can make the orchestra play.

Does that ever feel restrictive?

Yes it can feel restrictive. Depending on the conductor and your relationship with them, it can also be the most glorious, creative, stimulating and addictive experience. The only reason I have continued to do opera is that I find working with music absolutely thrilling. Theatre is quite scary for me sometimes because there is no music. You have to make all the music yourself.

How do you handle those kinds of negotiations with the conductor?

It depends. It's a question of who you're working with and, in essence, it's a human negotiation like any other. But everything is made more difficult because opera is an entirely international business, which means that you're very rarely in the same place as your collaborators. You have to arrange to meet on Zoom or you have to travel to see them conduct something and then make a meeting to sit down with the score. Music people have really, really packed schedules. They operate very differently from theatre people because they sing and play and conduct concerts. Somebody might be rehearsing an opera for six weeks in Amsterdam or wherever, but actually they need to leave early on the Thursday night because they've got a concert in Rome on the Friday and another recital in Perugia on Saturday and then they fly back to Amsterdam on Sunday to rehearse again on Monday. That's a genuinely common working schedule. Opera people don't think quite in the same way as theatre people do about process, because they've so rarely been involved in creating something from nothing.

Music is a language, so it helps tremendously to sit down with a conductor, go through the score and insist on unpicking the bits you know you want help with or think you want to cut. You want to understand how the conductor hears and sees the music. For example, when I was first directing Donizetti's *L'elisir d'amore* at Glyndebourne, I was fortunate enough to be working with a conductor called Enrique Mazzola who is passionate about the *bel canto* canon. He explained to me really precisely the subtle harmonic shifts, repeats and tempo changes which, because we were dealing with comic music, meant I could construct a great gag that would tie in exactly with that moment.

Do you get any say over which conductors you work with? In theatre you would get to choose your lighting designer or your sound designer but if you're employed by an opera company do you get to select the conductor in a similar way?

No. It's very unusual to get any choice, in fact it's normally the other way around – the conductor wouldn't want to work with a director who's going to be insensitive to their tastes. When you have a good relationship with a company you trust them not to pair you with someone unsuitable.

Another important factor with directing opera, though, is that it's planned so far in advance. I will get asked to do something three years from now, or possibly more. That's how the business operates because the musicians, the singers, the conductor must be booked so far ahead. This means the director is probably one of the slightly later considerations. I do have some say in terms of casting singers but not exclusively; it must be also agreed with the conductor because, technically, he is choosing a voice. I'm choosing a person. With the good conductor–director relationships you can talk about these things in a creative and holistic way. Also, as you get older, you realise it doesn't matter if you think so-and-so is perfect to play a role; if the voice isn't right, it's not going to work. The voice is the primary mode of expression in opera. It's not the only mode, but it trumps everything. It also depends very much on the repertoire. For example, I was once working on Puccini's *La bohème*, which is an Italian opera with these big love duets. If the singers singing Mimi and Rodolfo cannot transport the audience vocally, it doesn't matter how wonderful an actor I think they are, or what lovely people to work with they are. If they can't master those duets musically, you haven't got an opera. And I have lived this most painfully where I had two casts for *La bohème*. There was the Mimi I loved because I thought she was a marvellous actress. She could sing it, of course, but she didn't quite have the quality the audience expects from Puccini. There's a particular kind of liquidity of tone the music demands. She had a more modern voice, more suited to different kinds of repertoire, which I found thrilling. But put in front of a big house full of people and it was my other Mimi, the one who was so difficult to work with and who drove me absolutely wild, that the audience lapped up. Now, I can't say that one was the better singer, but the one who was right for the role was the one with the vocal quality that chimed with the music of Puccini and the conductor's interpretation. Had I had a different conductor who was much less conventional, it might have worked differently. It's a chemical process. It was sad for me because I liked my Mimi much better, but I could tell the audience didn't.

What do you do if you have a performer who is fantastic vocally but isn't, shall we say, a great actor? Or even a good actor?

That's what you learn through experience. Ideally, you want them to be able to do everything, and the great ones can. It's incredibly demanding, physically, mentally, emotionally and technically, singing opera. So the really great singers tend also to be pretty good actors, because they understand the music and that stimulates so much creativity. If they've got very flexible vocal technique, they tend to also be flexible in their imaginations and their bodies – it all goes together.

However, you do get singers who can't move much or aren't used to being asked to move. Sometimes that is because they have created a self-image whereby they don't move or they don't act. I usually approach that by working with the person and trying to give them as much time and support as I can. Sometimes you have to shock them a little or you have to challenge them. Nearly always, it's not true people can't act or can't move – or only to a certain point – and the real problem is their self-image. They've set limits on themselves, and your job as a director is to remove those limits and to take people to places they've perhaps not been, or not been for a long time.

Neurological studies have shown that when an opera singer is performing, the amount of brain activity surpasses top sportspeople, actors, pretty much anybody, because you're asking for a very, very high degree of fine motor skill with the vocal cords, combined with gross motor skills like breathwork and moving around. It took me a long time to really understand what that means but, in practice, it means it's much better to work through action and, vitally, to tie all action to the music. This doesn't mean you do every single thing on the beat or something, it's not that simple. But you need to also appreciate that many opera singers will be working in their third language – they might be Georgian, singing Italian and talking to me in English – and the words they are singing have become totally linked to the music in their heads. The real skill is for them to also be able to think and feel the words they are singing. So, if someone is not a 'good actor' I will do exercises more familiar to actors. There are so many ways to inhabit the words and to play a situation. Singers often struggle to connect with their text because they are so tied to the notes. But you must persevere and try to make them see that they're not just opera-machines, they're people telling a story.

When you add in those gross motor skills by asking singers to also move in certain ways or perform particular actions, does that ever interfere with their ability to sing?

No, that's a myth. There are a few things that are true. For example, if you want to hold a long and still note, it is very difficult to do it while you're running. It's also annoying for a singer to do things that are the director's clever idea but have absolutely no relationship to the spirit of the music. Lots of singers have been in very director-centred productions where they don't know why they're halfway up a ladder wearing a blue patent-leather spaceman outfit. But that's what they've been told to do and, as professionals, they are going to do it. I had a long Zoom call with a singer who was trying to sing Violetta from *La traviata* in a very abstract production where she was climbing the walls, literally. She said, 'I'm finding it difficult because he's not talked to me at all about the role. It's just all about climbing up and down these walls, and I'm really uncomfortable.' So I thought, okay, Violetta, she's dying of tuberculosis. And you're climbing the walls – it's his metaphor: you're climbing the walls. So, the wall is your illness. And you have to work with that as best you can.

The other thing you need to remember about opera is that there's a different level of fear to theatre. It's like being a trapeze artist: if you miss it, you miss it. And, what's more, if you miss that note, we can all hear it. Worse still, God forbid, is that you lose the conductor, and the orchestra is going along, but you've lost the tempo. It's simply terrifying. It's also strange and physically demanding because the singers can't always hear everything. The sound onstage is very odd and sometimes they can't hear anything at all while producing this huge sound, which makes them totally visually reliant on the conductor and on signals from each other.

Is that fear added to by audiences and critics? I have this perception of opera audiences and critics as being even harsher than theatre ones.

There is an element of what you say that's true, but I'm not so sure overall. There are still critics who clearly have no conception of what they're watching and are just interested in the music, or have very old-fashioned theatrical views. But it is changing. I think in essence it's just about the sheer demands of the thing itself. Opera is highly competitive. Yes, theatre's competitive, but your voice is a very mysterious thing, and a singer is very vulnerable. If you've got a cold, you can still do *King Lear*, just a bit croakily. But if you've got a cold, you can't sing opera. Then you lose your fee, which means there's an economic basis for the fear as well. I've known singers who have changed vocally enormously. It might be that you last worked with someone three years ago and then you're working with them again and notice a profound difference and someone whispers to you, 'Oh, she got divorced last year.' A voice is a difficult and emotional thing.

Does that awareness that you're working with a huge amount of fear and vulnerability ever become, on a human level in the rehearsal room, difficult to manage?

Those levels of vulnerability and fear are very rarely acknowledged. Often they're covered with what people call being diva-ish, which is a blend of what appears to be entitlement and laziness. They know the role; they've sung it before. That's much harder to work with. I don't find fear and vulnerability hard at all, I think it's a very creative place to be. What's difficult is when you're working with someone who has won this-and-that international singing competition, they have a big agent and they're going to go and sing this role at the Met in six months' time. And they know everything. That's difficult because it produces very boring performances. You have to judge carefully how you're going to open that person up. You can have the same bad behaviour from actors, but in opera you have so little time to unpick that behaviour. You can't do a great deal without the music, and in order to have the music you're not alone in the rehearsal room. You have a pianist, a vocal coach, a language coach and, hopefully, you've got the conductor, although normally it's their assistant in rehearsals. And the assistant conductor will, hopefully, know things like what the agreement is about the breathing and a whole host of other information which is not in my control. It all means I'm not alone in forging a relationship with a singer, which is a different thing to when you're a director in theatre working with an actor.

That concept of ceding control is quite different to working in theatre. Are there any aspects of that which you enjoy?

The balance between collaboration and control is there whether you're directing opera or theatre. The difference with opera is that everything is more extreme. One of my favourite opera stories comes from when I was working with the lovely American tenor David Kuebler. We'd had a hell of a ride; it'd been really tough. And he was watching some of the final rehearsals from the stalls, in full costume with his feet up. I was tearing my hair out because there were all sorts of things wrong. He looked over and he said, 'You know what I love about opera? It's like the lottery. Most of the time you lose, but when you win, you win big.' And that is what it's like. Wagner called opera a *Gesamtkunstwerk* because it unites all the art forms: music, dance, movement, text, acting, lighting and, now, even video and installation work. So, of course, you've got an enormous amount that can go wrong. And it's on a very big scale most of the time. If you're in a small late-eighteenth-century theatre made entirely of wood and you're doing Mozart, that's wonderful because it's intimate. If you're doing grand opera to four thousand people, it's a different ballgame.

How do you, as the director, manage the fear of that?

You just get better at it – or not! The fact is, at a certain point, you have to live with whatever it is that you have created. If you go and watch your own production and realise you got the set wrong, it's painful but there's nothing you can do about it. Absolutely nothing. There is no flexibility at that stage. Everyone agreed on the set and signed it off eighteen months ago. It's tough but you live with it, you move on, and you become quite tough with yourself about it. The other great thing about opera is that, come what may, the orchestra will play the music and the performers will sing it and they won't stop. So, at a certain point, you just accept: 'I've done what I've done and it is what it is.'

Jenny Sealey

Reimagining the aesthetic of access and organised chaos

Jenny Sealey has been the Artistic Director of Graeae Theatre since 1997. While with the company, the award-winning director has pioneered a new theatrical language and mode of creating theatre, which artistically embeds access requirements into shows. This has included the use of creative captioning, bilingual British Sign Language and spoken English stagings, and the innovative use of live audio description. Graeae are considered industry leaders for their work with Deaf, disabled and neurodivergent artists. Sealey's work as a director for the company includes *Reasons to be Cheerful* (2010), *The Threepenny Opera* (2014), *Blood Wedding* (2015) and *The House of Bernarda Alba* (2017).

'My ever-growing fear is "out of sight, out of mind".'

You've been at the helm of Graeae, one of the UK's most unique and significant theatre companies, for twenty-six years now. Since you became the Artistic Director, what major changes have you overseen?

Since I've been at Graeae, it's gone from being a very small company touring black-box theatres around the country to being a major player on Britain's main stages and internationally. We have a new-writing team, a creative learning team, three associate directors and a trainee producer. Simply put, we're a big company and a real force to be reckoned with. But the biggest thing we've done is change the landscape of British theatre by pioneering the aesthetic of access and working out how to embed live audio description, sign language and creative captioning into the fabric of a production. The journey to doing that started with Ewan Marshall, my predecessor, who integrated interpreters, so I built on that by exploring creative captioning and introducing live and pre-recorded audio description. When we discovered the theatrical richness of access as a company, it was a huge turning point. We started doing it with every single show we made and now mainstream companies across the world are adapting the same practices into their work. So, it's not too bold a claim to say that we have transformed the landscape of how people can make theatre. For us, it has also always been about placing Deaf and disabled people centre-stage, and that mission hasn't changed in the forty years since the company started. The thing that's changed is that more companies are now also doing it, but they do it some of the time and we do it all the time – that's the key difference.

Take me back to the very beginning. In your wildest imagination, what did you hope Graeae would become with you in charge?

In my interview I had to do a presentation, and in it I said that at some point in the next ten years, Graeae will be at the Royal Shakespeare Company doing *Romeo and Juliet*. So far, we haven't been invited to the RSC, but we are currently in conversation with other major venues about doing Shakespeare. The point, however, was that I knew we needed to be on those big stages. I thought that was really important because it's about visibility. Throughout history, disabled people have been hidden. And Graeae is about not hiding us: we are here. So, what I said in that original presentation was that we needed to be on small stages, medium-sized stages, big stages – we needed to be absolutely everywhere because my ever-growing fear is 'out of sight, out of mind'. Which is why we are present on so many different platforms, whether that's online, in schools, in colleges, in universities, in the theatre, in writing seminars. It's just to remind people that disabled people have a right to be part of the cultural fabric of society.

I also knew that there is a real lack of training opportunities for Deaf and disabled artists. The first job the board asked me to do was to look at the gaps in training. From doing that, I realised drama schools weren't overly interested in training us because they didn't think there were enough jobs for us. And when someone says, 'No, you can't do that', I go, 'Yes we can, but we'll do it ourselves.' Which was exactly what we did. We set up the Missing Piece training course and ran it for three years on our own and then for two years with London Metropolitan University. We then realised that, as a theatre company, we couldn't do everything ourselves and the drama schools themselves needed to take responsibility to make their training accessible. To some extent it's worked, although we're still in a position where we feel we need to oversee training opportunities because the existing ones only provide opportunities for one or two people. We have good relationships with Rose Bruford, LAMDA, RADA and Central School of Speech and Drama, but we still need there to be more offered and provided. It's very, very isolating to be the only disabled person on a course. I was the only Deaf person at Middlesex University, which meant the onus was on me to find ways to cope. I had to sort it all out myself with no support. A lot of the disabled people we know who are at drama school struggle. But when there are more of you, you have allies, and you make a bigger impact. And, gradually, people start to get it.

And from that original vision and presentation, does the company now resemble what you sketched out? Or has it evolved into something else?

The company continues to evolve, which is why I've been at Graeae so long. The challenges are varied and ever-changing. Since I've been there, there has been the challenge of setting up actor training, the challenge of playing around with the aesthetic of access; and the challenge of having our own building. We've now got this beautiful bespoke building on the Kingsland Road with rehearsal space and our offices, but getting that set up was another big challenge. And then, in recent years, there was the challenge of the pandemic. And there's always been the challenge of battling with the mainstream world and advocating for real social change.

All of our productions are so different because of the artists we employ, so nothing we make can pigeonhole us as a company. The only consistent thing is that we will endeavour to find the right artistic aesthetic to make the work accessible. We also continue to learn by our mistakes, and we continue to make mistakes because access and the world of disability are huge. Part of how we learn is through people being much more confident to talk about, for example, neurodiversity and how they work best. What's accessible for one person is not for another, so we're having to constantly refine and redefine our working practice. It's exciting, exhausting and terrifying, which keeps me fuelled! You can't rest on your laurels and say, 'Hooray! We know what we're doing!' Because we don't. I love the fact that we're a real learning company and we're constantly sharing what we learn. We shout out as loudly about our mistakes and our fuck-ups as we do our successes.

With respect to 'what works for one person doesn't work for another', when you're in charge of a rehearsal room where there

are a lot of different people with a lot of different access needs, what practical measures do you use to address that?

We do an access audit with everybody in which we ask what access provision they would prefer to have in the rehearsal room. We then go about making that provision. So, for example, I have a sign language interpreter for me. We also have a general access worker in the rehearsal room who can work with the whole team, from doing small things like making tea and coffee and making sure the room is kept accessible and tidy, to more specific access-related requirements. Each performer and artist is different, but we'll often have note-takers, line-readers, audio-describing line-feeders and more. The important thing is making sure that everyone understands why everyone is there and what their role is. Sometimes we work with performers who don't realise what their access needs are until halfway through a rehearsal period, but we respond to requests at any stage and try to make things happen.

Irrespective of what access requirements you have in place, do you have practices or techniques that you always use in the rehearsal space, whoever the performers are and whatever the show is that's being created?

I play Zip Zap Boing all the time. Every single time. I also do name signs, but outside of those two things, every rehearsal process is different. It really is. The only constant is that I always have a certain level of chaos – or so I've been told! I don't think I run a typical rehearsal room. It all depends on what the show is and who my stage-management and creative teams are. For instance, with the opera I am currently working on, I've been sharing the space with a music director who will take music rehearsals while I concentrate on staging the show. Then, with the musical *Reasons to be Cheerful*, I worked with a fantastic Deaf choreographer called Mark Smith. Again, we shared rehearsals so that sometimes the cast were working on movement and dance with him, and sometimes on acting with me. Occasionally, that meant he was saying he needed more time with them and sometimes I was saying the same, but we made it work really nicely. Overall, I don't have a template other than to say that access is everyone's responsibility. I also ask people to inform me if they need to have time out or are feeling overwhelmed and need to sit down for a bit. I don't want to kill anyone in the process. The work will get done but not at the expense of completely burning somebody out. We run our rehearsal rooms through kindness, support and rigour.

Could you say a little bit more about what you mean by 'chaos' when used to describe your rehearsal room?

I think there are some directors who like to sit around the table and action a play. I can't stand doing that. I'm not clever enough to do it and I don't like doing it. I like to find things out by actors just throwing themselves in, moving around and trying things out. It's only through doing that that I figure out what works. It also means the actors inform the process. I don't want to be one of the directors who I worked with as a co-director who were like, 'I want you to walk forward on that line' or, 'Say it like that.' I find the shape of a show through playing around with different thoughts and ideas and pictures. And only through doing that do I start to know what else needs to be done and how. I mean, of course I will come to a rehearsal with some ideas already. But I like to see what the actors come up with themselves because often actors have better ideas than I do. I don't actually think it is chaotic, but I use the word 'chaos' because I know some people – particularly if they're neurodiverse – do think it is. Some people like there to be structure and detail present from the very beginning. Whereas, for me, the structure comes later.

From an artistic perspective, have changes to the available technology meant that you can now do things with embedding access that you weren't previously able to?

Very much so. For my first-ever captioned show, we used a PowerPoint that I'd made with my access manager Claire – we pretty much just pasted it all together. But what we can do with creative captioning now, like having words running down the page or across the page or whatever, it's so much more fun. Lots of companies, including us, are now being playful with creative captioning. It's very exciting.

Where sign language is concerned, I've always had the interpreters as a character within the work – they're a part of everything, not just a person who stands by the side of the stage and interprets for the audience. In *Reasons to be Cheerful*, we embedded the audio description into the piece by having the audio describer on stage speaking quietly down a 1970s payphone to blind audience members. We included a joke wherein they were 'on the phone to blind Derek'. Other characters could then come up to the phone and give a description of, for example, their costume and everyone knew that 'blind Derek' was getting a blow-by-blow description of what was going on onstage. The sound design included the noise of the coins going into the payphone, and it was those beautiful little moments of detail that added to the work as a whole. It's changes to the tech available that allows us to do clever things like this although, of course, there's so much more we could be doing as well.

For the opera I'm working on, we've been creating a sonogram of the whole piece, which represents the flow of the music. We're also making a whole tactile work for blind audience members and an immersive experience for Deaf-blind audience members, which includes things like trying on costumes, so they can completely experience the opera. We'll also be briefing their Deaf-blind guides. We've only done a tiny bit of work with Deaf-blind audiences so far, so that's a journey we're just starting out on with help from an amazing Deaf-blind consultant. In terms of technology, there are new vibrating things that can tell you where the music is. I tried one myself and I'm not initially a fan, but I've only done it once and want to investigate it further. We're working with Drake Music Scotland, who make adapted instruments for disabled people, to learn about their experiences around the visceral experience of music. As with everything, finding out who we can work with and learn from is a big part of our own research.

When you've experimented with embedding access and using new techniques or technology in the past, have there been things you've tried that didn't work out?

One mistake we've made time and time again is assuming that a blind audience member has the time to arrive at the theatre early to listen to the preamble, which is a synopsis of the show and an introduction to the characters. Because why should a blind audience member have to turn up fifteen minutes earlier? That's not equitable. We do put stuff on our website but, again, that's assuming everyone has the time and means to access that in advance. So instead, I'm working on always embedding a framework where the actors introduce themselves and say a little bit about their costume and other information when they're on stage. But I'm still working out the exact best way to do this. When we did *The House of Bernarda Alba* at Manchester Royal Exchange, we received feedback from a blind audience member that the audio description was so seamlessly written into the narrative that it didn't necessarily inform people well enough as to what was happening visually on stage. Partly because it was almost too smart, in a way. It read like text rather than having that slightly heightened thing that's needed for somebody to be able to know that's what's happening on stage.

We haven't ever done the all-singing, all-dancing, completely-and-utterly accessible show. We haven't. But we are fuelled by that as a mission. One problem is that what's accessible for one blind person isn't for another. For example, when we did an amazing piece called *This Is Not for You* with wounded disabled veterans, the audio description was quite sparse because it was a music-heavy piece and there was so much happening on stage. And some people thought the audio description was too sparse and some felt it was enough. So how do you get it right? We do always have blind advisers and BSL consultants to help us get more right than wrong, but, like I said, we have never got it completely right, ever. And maybe we never will.

Rachel O'Riordan

Empathy and the alchemical capacity between audience and actor

Rachel O'Riordan became the Artistic Director of the Lyric Hammersmith Theatre, London, in 2019. Prior to this, the award-winning Irish theatre director was Artistic Director of the Sherman Theatre in Cardiff. Her period in charge saw the theatre's status within the industry rise exponentially, turning it into one of the most admired producing theatres in the UK. Her work is characterised by a bleakly beautiful aesthetic, and she has a long-running collaboration with the Welsh playwright Gary Owen. The pair's work includes *Iphigenia in Splott* (2015/16), *Killology* (2017) and *Romeo and Julie* (2023).

'An auditorium is a place where people come to have their hearts broken.'

From the point where I first started watching your work at the Sherman Theatre in Cardiff through to now, I've been struck by how almost all of it deals with what some would consider 'heavy' themes – there's a lot of grief, pain, trauma and violence in there, along with real emotional heft. So my first question is simply: what draws you to plays with this type of content?

You've noticed something that I haven't been conscious of, but, thinking about it, I can see that you're right. Because even with the comedy *Love, Love, Love* by Mike Bartlett – which I directed at the Lyric Hammersmith in 2020 – I remember the playwright saying to me that no one had ever directed it like a straight play before. And I think he meant, in particular, the divorce scene. People, he said, normally play it for laughs, whereas I thought, 'This is fucking heartbreaking.' So I directed it as heartbreaking.

I feel that an auditorium is a place where people come to have their hearts broken in a way that makes them understand themselves better. And sometimes there is a great relief in seeing one's own pain on the stage because – if it's done right – that is cathartic. But it's interesting you point this out because I've never consciously said to myself, 'I want to put plays on stage that are about trauma or pain.' But I do know that the reason I'm a director is that I believe that theatre has this kind of alchemical capacity between audience and actor, which is about a profound creation of empathy and understanding in the space that exists between those watching and those performing – whether that space is an auditorium or a field, or a pub.

As an artistic director, I'm somebody who enjoys bringing everyone together into a shared space. It's quite possible you have a completely different lived experience to the person you end up sitting next to, but for this brief period you're in the same place at the same time, watching the same thing. And if the material is powerful enough to affect both of you at the same time, that's just extraordinary, because there's something that's created in an auditorium, when it's really cooking, that is about a shared empathy created by the energy. We've all been in auditoria like that and had the feeling that this space, in this moment, is like nothing else. And that's what I try and do every time I direct.

So maybe that guides me towards the material rather than the other way around, because I know what I believe theatre's for, which is the creation of empathy despite difference. I also think the theatre itself is a conduit for a disparity of opinion and experience, with everything that is in the auditorium being channelled together and filtered through what is on stage.

I remember, for example, when we took Gary Owen's *Iphigenia in Splott* to New York in 2017, it was so interesting to notice the difference in audience reaction to the play from an American audience rather than a British one. I think because they don't have the NHS in America, there was a feeling that Effie, the main character, should stop complaining and get a job, so although they understood it intellectually it didn't engender the same rage that it did when it was performed in Wales, or especially in London in 2022. And, to me, that's fascinating. That's the point. I don't want the same reaction all the time and I don't want the same audience all the time. I don't want to say, 'This theatre is for this sort of person.' That's absolutely the opposite of what I believe in. I think all theatres are houses for everyone.

Talking of audience reaction, when you have a play on – especially if it's at the theatre where you are the artistic director – how often do you watch it during a run and, specifically, do you take note of audience reaction? And would you make changes to a play if, say, an audience was getting bored at a certain point or not reacting the way you wanted them to react?

Oh yes, definitely. In answer to your first question of how often I go in, the answer would probably be: not often enough. I don't enjoy seeing my own work, so were it not for the fact I love seeing the actors perform and love to support them, I would probably choose never to see my own work again once it's on! I feel like it's the equivalent of an author sitting down to read their own novel or a painter going to a gallery to see their own painting – why would you do that?! I also primarily see a director's job as being in the rehearsal room. That's where I excavate the play and discover what my take on it is, but once I've found that and it's on stage, it's the audience's job to celebrate and respond to it.

However, part of my job, especially as an AD, is paying attention to audiences and how they are reacting. There's a lot you can fix in previews if, for example, there's a bit where the audience are losing focus. Actors' work evolves and it's quite normal to find something has changed over the course of the run and you need to recalibrate it.

The reason I make theatre is for the audience. My idea of making 'bad theatre' would be if nothing happened in the auditorium and everyone was sitting there like they were almost dead. In fact, if an audience is completely passive, I don't feel I've done my job right.

You said that you see your job as being inside the rehearsal room. Do you tend to arrive at rehearsals with a clear idea of what the play is, what its emotions are and how you're going to direct it? Or does that all come out during the rehearsal period, shaped by the actors and the other people who are there with you?

Both. If I didn't have any sense of the feeling of the play in the first place, I probably wouldn't direct it. For me to direct a play, I have to have a strong feeling about it. I'll usually read a play and, if it's something I should direct, I'll have a very immediate response.

But my absolute favourite thing is working with actors to open up portal after portal in themselves and in a play. The way I do that is to work in layers, so we'll normally do a rough staging of the whole piece very, very quickly. And then we'll go back and dig in a little deeper. And then we'll go back and dig in deeper still, and keep repeating that process until – depending on how long we have in rehearsals – it's something we feel is exciting and new.

One thing I never, ever do is ask personal questions. I never ask about anyone's history and never have done, even when I was younger. I don't think it's fair and, in fact, it can be really dangerous. So everything is channelled through the script. I would never say, 'How does this relate to something you've experienced?' I'm not a trained psychologist and most other directors aren't either, so why ask a question when you're not equipped to deal with the potential answer? But sometimes an actor will, of their own accord, bring up something in their life that relates to the material and then we can talk about that if they want to.

Do you also talk to the actors about how it potentially affects them to be performing very emotionally intense material? For example, performing Gary Owen's *Iphigenia in Splott* or *Killology*, night after night, is a big thing to do...

Yes, absolutely. I actually talked more to Sophie Melville about *Iphigenia* than the three guys performing *Killology*, partly because they had each other to talk to. We didn't have any formal emotional support for Sophie, but we spent a lot of time talking about the world and the character and all the things that had shaped her. There were also certain ways I went about directing the play to help alleviate some of the stress of it. For example, we didn't immediately do it all in one go. I shaped the process so that we weren't going to come in on day one and go in hard on it straight away.

But Sophie was so brilliant in it. There is a part, near the end, that even now I can't remember without crying – it's seared into my sense memory. It's right at the end when her baby has died and she's given up on the idea of compensation, and she says, 'And still you see me walking home pissed at night and you think: stupid skank, dirty slag... ' Then she looks at the audience. And I will never, ever forget the feeling I had in the audience whenever that moment happened. It was really uncomfortable but exactly what I wanted to say with the piece. It's one of the things I'm most proud of ever being involved with.

When you're working with an actor like Sophie Melville, do you get a similar feeling when casting them as you would reading a play for the first time, in terms of just knowing there is something special about them?

Often, yes.

And what is that 'thing'?

That's a good question! I'm not a director who always works with the same actors, which I think is important because, ultimately, you're an employer and it's not fair. But I think the people I'm drawn to cast have grit in them. Their inner engine is 'on' and, often but not always, they are working class. I don't have a policy on that, but it seems to be something that often happens. Maybe because, in an audition situation, I'm drawn to a certain hunger. I think it's also because when I started directing, I was working in Belfast with a lot of actors who were very different to, let's say, a lot the actors who are working in London today. I don't know quite what it is, but I think there is something about the hunger and the drive people like that have that I connect with.

When you've cast those actors and you step inside the rehearsal space with them, do the characteristics of each different group shape the process you then use to create a piece of theatre? Or do you have a set way of working that you return to again and again?

Yes, they do. Apart from starting with a week spent around the table delving into the text, I don't have any set routines or practices that I return to repeatedly. When I was starting out, I kind of thought I needed to develop a 'method'. So I used to do all kinds of things like hour-long warm-ups and stuff. But I don't do that any more.

However, I do think it is the director's job to provide some clarity for the performers. I'm not of the school of thought where the actors will be asking themselves what is going on and I'll be like, 'Hey, guys, I don't know, let's find it together!' I don't think that's fair. So I do have a vision for it – and that's a vision that can and should change during the rehearsal process. But I believe you need to have something clear to offer on day one. For example, when I was directing Conor McPherson's *The Seafarer* at Perth Theatre in 2013, I said on day one of rehearsals, 'This is not a secular play. The devil is real. It's not an allegory.' And they're like, 'Oh!' Because I think they'd all interpreted it as if it was. And I said, 'Mr Lockhart is not a metaphor for the devil. He *is* the devil.' And that was non-negotiable. And everyone was really excited by that. Because, of course, it's hard to play a metaphor if you're an actor! It raised the stakes in the room – I could feel people in the room going 'think, think, think' and 'rethink, rethink, rethink', and that was thrilling to be around.

Has the way you communicate with actors changed over the years? And, if so, has that change been deliberate?

It probably has, but not consciously. I think sometimes I do it better than at others. It's not always worked, and I haven't always had the perfect relationship with every actor I have worked with. But I have a lot of admiration for all actors and the courage of what they do. And I think I bring that attitude into the room with me. When I direct an actor, I want them to give the best performance they have ever done in their career. And I will just say that to them sometimes. My job is to make them realise that their capacity for brilliance is bigger than they imagined. And if I can do that, and then connect them to the text, then that connects to the audience.

And when it all finishes, do you have any specific routines or debrief processes to mark the close of a show?

At the Lyric Hammersmith, we do debrief in-house. But with the actors, no, we just go and have a drink together on the last night. I'm old-school in that way, I will always make it my business to be at the last show to see it out, because it's tradition and it's good manners. It's important for me and the actors to say goodbye to it because theatre is such an ephemeral thing. You have to mark that moment, if possible, and honour the fact that, unlike with a novel or painting, you're probably not going to see it ever again.

When you're working on a show – especially as we started out talking about the kind of work you make – does it invade your whole life? For instance, do you feel like you're constantly living with it? Do you dream of it?

Yes, yes, yes!

And does that ever feel like 'too much'? Do you ever just want to shut off for the weekend?

Yes! But we can't. So you don't. I mean, there is probably a more modern way of answering that question…

Like, 'Oh, I go for a run…'

Well, I do go for a run! But I still think about it. And, yes, I do dream about it. I think about it obsessively. When I'm in rehearsals, I think about it all weekend. My soul and my brain don't know it's Saturday or Sunday, however much I tell them it is. You can't switch that off; you kind of have to accept it. And then rest afterwards.

Is that particularly difficult when you're balancing directing a play with being an artistic director? You know, if you have to come out of rehearsal and say, 'Okay, now we're going to talk about the toilets'?

Being an artistic director who directs is all-consuming, and I'm not sure I can see a way of it not being so. But it's such a great honour to be allowed to be one, and to be trusted to be one, that I don't, as much as it's tiring, ever genuinely mind any part of it. It's a life choice, to do this. It's nothing less than that.

Does it all feel a bit addictive? Like you get to the end of one show and then have to start another one?

I think there's probably something in that. I mean, otherwise, why else would you do the job – logically speaking? Press night is so stressful, and doubly when you're an AD, that you're always tempted to ask, 'Why am I doing this?!' But there's something that feels so important in acting that you end up thinking, 'Well, I've thrown my hat into the ring now.' It's who I am, and I just keep going, trying not to fuck it up and trying to do right by people. That's the essence of what I do: I try to do right by people, I try to do right by artists, and I try to do right by everyone who works here at the Lyric Hammersmith. I'm not sure I get it right all the time. But I try to do that with my whole heart. And that's it.

Tinuke Craig

Playing games and putting character first

Tinuke Craig first came to the attention of critics and audiences as the winner of the Genesis Future Directors Award in 2014, which led to her directing debbie tucker green's *dirty butterfly* at the Young Vic. Since then, she has directed a number of aesthetically bold plays and musicals at theatres across the UK, including Sarah Kane's *Crave* at Chichester Festival Theatre (2020), *The Color Purple* at Leicester Curve and Birmingham Hippodrome, followed by a national tour (2019) and *Jitney* at Leeds Playhouse (2021), which transferred to the Old Vic in 2022 and was also followed by a national tour.

'There's this feeling that "being a director" means sitting there drawing lines on a script...'

When I previously interviewed you ahead of your pantomime, *Cinderella*, opening at the Lyric Hammersmith in 2019, we spoke about meticulously digging into a text – looking at it line by line and analysing the subtext and so on. Is that still a big part of your practice and your route into the play – through the words, essentially?

Yes, it is. Although I should start by saying that it's more about the characters than the words. I approach the text differently depending on whether I'm doing my own preliminary prep work or if I'm in the rehearsal room with the actors. I have a very short attention span and I tend to work in quite short bursts. When I first approach a script on my own, I find it useful to look for trends amongst the characters. For example: 'Why does she keep behaving like that?' Or: 'Why does he not behave the way you would expect him to?' I start to make note of things like the specific language one character will use with another but not with everyone else and ask, 'Why is that?'

When I'm working on a play that's more 'traditional' in its make-up, character and the relationships between characters becomes especially important to me. I spend a lot of time trying to imagine what it would be like to receive this play as an audience member: 'How is it making me feel? What parts am I most interested in? Where am I feeling bored?' I mean, hopefully I'm never really bored, but the truth is we often do feel bored when watching or reading plays, so where are those less-involving moments?

I start with quite an academic approach and set myself little tasks and little lists to write. If I'm totally unencumbered and just reading a play,

I often get distracted. So it's useful for me to have particular things in mind when reading it like: 'I'm going to read it again, the whole way though, and this time I'm going to look at what the character's relationship to the outside world is like.' Part of why I do that is to focus my brain, but it also enables me to start picking up on different themes, relationships and trends within the play.

Then, when I'm with the actors in the rehearsal room, the focus often shifts more to the text itself, because they are so fundamentally good at understanding and intuiting character for themselves. Often, I will share with them what I've learnt about character and because they're so brilliantly instinctive in response to that, we can then use the text as our kind of leverage through the rest of the script. That's when it becomes really useful to start combing through it line by line, because you start to spot little trends and you hear the whole thing differently when an actor is saying the lines out loud.

So, the short answer is: Yes, I still focus a lot on the script! And the longer answer is: When I'm doing my own prep, the focus is more on the characters and the storyline, and I save line-by-line analysis for when the actors are in the rehearsal space.

Does that mean your rehearsal periods start with round-the-table work? Or do you go straight into something else, like working on movement?

It's probably a bit of both, which isn't a very satisfying answer! I find it hard to talk about my process because I'm not sure that I have one.

But that in itself is interesting…

I think, in all honesty, my process is dictated by the show I'm working on. I have done rehearsal processes where we've sat around the table for the whole of the first week, and I've done others where we've not sat down once. The play itself has a lot to do with whether we focus on table work or not. For example, when I directed Sarah Kane's *Crave* at the Chichester Festival Theatre in 2020, it didn't feel very useful to sit around the table because the text means both everything and absolutely nothing. And the one person, the playwright, who could have told us what it means, has passed away, and even if she was still with us, she probably wouldn't have told us either. So answering the basic question of 'What does it mean?' became kind of redundant. We did do a bit of table work, but we limited it to about an hour and a half per day, when we would sit down and read a bit and share our thoughts on it, or any feelings, or point out any repetitions or trends, or things that we were particularly interested in. But, ultimately, it was much more useful to get the play on its feet and try things out. We knew, for example, that we were going to use treadmills in the production, but we did a lot of rehearsals where we performed it completely differently. We played out scenes where everyone was running around the entire space, or lying on the floor, or getting really close to each other, or staying far apart.

Then, when I directed Maxim Gorky's *Vassa* at the Almeida Theatre in 2019, we spent a lot of time at the table because, simply, there were lots of things to learn, like the historical background and culturally specific Russian references.

But if there is one thing I consistently do, it's that I try to mix up and vary the activities in the room a lot. One of the strategies I've developed in connection to my own concentration span and ADHD is to compartmentalise the schedule, a bit like when you have a timetable in school. So, for example, if we do table work in the morning, I will make sure we are doing a movement session in the afternoon. Or if we're doing a voice session another morning, I'll then move on to some scene work. I plan it out quite carefully, with timings like: from 10 a.m. to 12 p.m. we will be doing this… and so on throughout the day, so that I'm dealing with things in bite-sized chunks.

So far, I've found this approach – although designed to accommodate my own attention span – also works well with actors because it helps keep the room and the process quite alive. And, of course, there is always flexibility built in: if we're on a roll with something, I can just say, 'Okay, we're sticking with this for now', and if we're not really finding something exciting then hopefully the next thing we move on to will work better.

When I was working on my first couple of plays, I did a lot of sitting around a table, mostly because I thought that was what you were 'supposed' to do as a director. It's like drawing uniting lines on a script; there's this feeling that 'being a director' means sitting there drawing lines on a script, whereas now I almost never do that – it's just not that helpful to me.

The other thing I would say is that my process changes hugely depending on the kind of actors who are in the room with me. When I say 'kind' of actors, I mean their personalities and sensibilities, and experience levels and relationship to the play. If I'm working with a group who are mega-intuitive, it's not very useful to spend ages at the table. Or, if I have actors who simply aren't very nourished by table work and making them do it feels like a kind of punishment or like we're all in school, then I quickly switch to getting the whole thing on its feet with people running around. But there are some actors who need the time around the table, and they need it because it helps them form a really good foundation to the play – maybe they're people who are a little bit more analytical or academic in the way that they work. In that scenario, it's not fair for me to say, 'Let's just do it all on the fly!'

I understand my job as being about putting actors in a position where they can do their best work, and I can't expect them to do that if I'm not giving them a process that's useful to them. I'm sure if you asked actors I have worked with, they would say, 'Oh, Tinu? She always does *x*, *y* and *z*...' But I'm not sure I'd be able to name what those things are. The only thing I know is that I always do a lot of character work, and a fair bit of improvisation connected to that, and forging clearly drawn and emotionally distinct characters.

What activities do you get the actors to do to help build that depth of character?

I get them to do a lot of writing. When I was about seventeen, I was on the Young Writers' course at the Royal Court. We were taught by the playwright Simon Stephens, and he does all these character exercises for writers which involve making loads of lists about a character. The lists will focus on things like: things everyone knows about this character, things nobody knows about this character, things the character secretly wants, things they want by the end of the day, or by the end of the week, or by the end of their lives, and so on. All these lists help writers form clear, distinct characters. I found that really useful at the time and I still use that technique now.

I get actors to write down lists about their characters and some of the things that inform the text. Sometimes that will be clear; for example, it might say in the script what a character's profession is. And other times, they'll have to infer things. I'm very happy for them to make stuff up and to include conjecture, as long as it doesn't contradict what we have on the page. It means actors come up with their own idea, rather than being dictated stuff by me, and then they own those views and ideas.

I also do improvisation tasks, including some long-form stuff. For example, we might work step by step through each hour of a character's day. Or we'll think about what their childhood was like. Or, if there's an important moment in the script where someone talks about a memory, we might act out that memory, even if it's not actually depicted in the script. We might also draw up family-tree connections and show how everyone in a play knows each other. When I worked on *Jitney* by August Wilson, that play involves a huge number of offstage characters, so we made a list of all those characters and then found possible images to match up with our idea of the character. It felt like a way of mentally keeping the community rich and also meant we could all visualise the same person when an offstage character was mentioned.

You mentioned Simon Stephens there, but have there been any theatre directors who have directly informed your way of working? Perhaps someone you assisted or observed when you were at an earlier point in your career?

Joe Hill-Gibbins is a huge influence on me. I assisted him at the Young Vic and one of the great things about working with Joe is that he really uses his assistants. He does extensive prep for all his shows and he involves his assistant in that right from the beginning. So, you start working with him about sixteen months before a show opens. That involves meeting up a couple of times a week, or whenever is possible, and talking about the show and going through certain aspects of it. It makes you feel like you are genuinely making a difference to how the production is taking shape and being helpful to him.

But, above all, what he demonstrated to me in the rehearsal room is this attitude of: 'Why not?' He's fearless about trying anything out, with the assumption that if it works then we'll figure out why it works later and if it doesn't, then that's not a problem. I still have this thing in rehearsals where I'll sometimes feel the need to be a bit apologetic. I'll be like, 'Um... so I've got this idea for a dance and we can try this out because it works for this reason, but if it doesn't work then we can scrap it, but I think it would be a lovely idea...' Whereas Joe would just be like, 'Would it be fun if they danced? Great! Let's dance!', and then if it worked, he'd say, 'Oh and it also works for this intellectual reason...' I think his approach works because it's just infinitely more positive, which helps get the actors on side, and it means you're brave, and try more things, even if they don't work out. I try very hard to hang on to that 'Why not?' quality.

Working with Joe also shaped how I think about the rehearsal room. My aim isn't to make a rehearsal room fun, but it is to make it feel free and unencumbered. Running a room that way suits me much better, whereas previously I had this idea that a rehearsal room should be quite a serious place, where everyone was having serious discussions about 'the craft' and things. I have a lot of respect for directors who run rooms like that, but I don't think my skills suit running a room like that. What I've been able to do more recently is to find a way of running a room that is a bit gentler and a bit more free-flowing. That might mean that we take more breaks, or we start the day by playing a game. I usually have a structure for the day in my head, so actors don't feel like they're freefalling, but that structure is malleable and includes moments when we'll simply follow our noses and see what feels most useful each day. Some actors love this way of working and others don't, but I think I've become much better at finding the actors in audition who do like it.

I think what Joe showed me was that, underneath this way of working that, on the surface, feels very loose and free, is actually a huge amount of rigour, thought and carefulness around the work. But he also just made me feel okay about running a room like that! It was kind of like being given permission to run a room that felt that way.

And in order to create that kind of environment what kind of, for instance, games would you get people up and playing?

I play lots of ball games, despite not being able to catch! If I have a big enough cast we will play Four Square, which is the classic. I also play Ball-in-the-Bucket, which I stole off Joe Hill-Gibbins, who I believe stole it off someone else in turn. So there's this lineage of rehearsal-room Ball-in-the-Bucket. It's essentially a game of keepy-uppy with the ball, where you kind of build an assault course in the rehearsal room and the company have to keep the ball in the air whilst they, for example, all go through a door and all put on hats and then come around the back and hit the ball on the wall and, finally, put the ball in the bucket. You play it competitively in teams and it's quite addictive; it has this video-game *Super Mario* quality of nearly making it before you die. Which I think is quite good for one's brain.

It's also useful because it gives you, as the director, ten minutes at the start of the day to just breathe and centre yourself in the room. Also, by observing the actors playing the game, you get to work out things about their personalities – like, 'He's competitive' or 'She's a bit more shy' – and then decide how you can best use and respond to those qualities.

I also play other games like Wah and Hep, which is like an ultra-sophisticated version of Zip Zap Boing, especially if I'm working in drama schools as the pupils are often really up for that. But, with professional shows, it depends on the cast a lot. Sometimes you have a cast who love playing games, and sometimes you try it out once and they all look at you like they want you to die, so you never go there again! Or sometimes, they seem reticent but you genuinely think it would be a good idea for them to persevere and so you press on with it – but only if you have a good reason to! Again, hopefully as you progress through your career, you become better at selecting the actors who will work well in your rehearsal room and really thrive.

Sarah Frankcom

Imposter syndrome and being the artist only you can be

Sarah Frankcom is an award-winning freelance theatre director who was the Artistic Director of the Manchester Royal Exchange from 2008 to 2019, before becoming Director of the London Academy of Music and Dramatic Art (LAMDA) from 2019 to 2021. Collaboration with actors and artists forms an important part of her practice and includes, famously, a long-running collaboration with the actress Maxine Peake, who has starred in productions including *Hamlet* (2014), *A Streetcar Named Desire* (2016) and *Happy Days* (2018). She is also known for working with the playwright Simon Stephens on multiple occasions. Her other significant work includes a much-lauded production of Thornton Wilder's *Our Town* (2017), staged in the wake of the Manchester bombing.

'I wasn't the kind of person who could just sit there.'

When directors discuss their route into theatre they often talk about formative experiences working as an assistant. I wanted to turn that subject around and, instead, ask you what it's like being a very experienced director working with an assistant? What is that relationship like and how can it benefit your practice?

It can be massively beneficial. For me, it's one of the most sustaining and evolving relationships, and one that changes your practice as a director. I've found that working with assistants has made me look at who I am and how I lead a room. An assistant can offer incredible insight when you're at your most vulnerable; they can give you information on how the entire collaborative process is going, including what others – actors and creatives – might be too nervous to say to the director. For the past ten years or so, I've placed an emphasis on learning from my assistants and allocating them quite a lot of responsibility. I see them as an integral part of the collaboration, not an afterthought. Traditionally, the assistant director was someone who looked after the show after the director had moved on to another project. But, for me, I want their creative brain in the rehearsal space as much as possible, because I'm a great believer that everything is much improved the more everybody feels they can put something into it. Every rehearsal has to be an opportunity to open as many windows and doors as you can. Because of that, I've actively sought out assistant relationships where people are really up for, and comfortable with, playing a big role in creating the work.

I also believe that, often, you're meeting the future when working with assistant directors. I've received some of my most amazing notes from assistant directors and I've had some of my most devastating notes from assistant directors. And I'm not only fine with that, but I also actually think that's amazing. It's hard to tell, sometimes, who is going to make a great director just by having a conversation with them. I'm very intrigued by shy and awkward people – because I am a shy and awkward person – and I've often been staggered when seeing someone at work who, previously, you didn't necessarily see as having the ability to be an amazing director in them and that suddenly being revealed. My only stipulation is that an assistant has to either be paid or be part of a formal training programme. I feel very strongly that having someone in the room who is not being paid creates a really bad situation.

When we exchanged emails prior to this conversation you described assistant directors as being 'often overlooked, misunderstood and scandalously paid'. Why do you think all these things are true?

Until relatively recently, the industry has been able to be very lazy about inclusivity and who is in the room. We've only just started having conversations about working practices and how bad they can be. To be an assistant or an associate director, you need to serve a vision and, because of that, I think it's a role that has been taken advantage of or mistreated – although sometimes in well-meaning ways. But the assistant is often the person whom the actors might feel most comfortable being vulnerable with; they're the ones who most frequently stay behind after rehearsals end to help actors learn their lines. Sometimes they're even the ones to go on stage if an actor is unwell, because we no longer really have an understudy system in this country. In short, we want them to do an awful lot – and I sometimes wonder why they don't complain more, because it's a really, really hard job to do.

During the pandemic, I remember interviewing Bryony Shanahan, who went on to be the co-Artistic Director at the Royal Exchange after you left, and she spoke about working as your assistant when she was first starting out. She recalled being given

the responsibility of running the entire room and that being both terrifying and brilliant, as a demonstration of someone having faith in her. Did you make a conscious decision to work with assistants in this way?

I think it depends on the assistant and where they are in their career. With Bryony, she had done a lot of assisting and I knew she needed to lead a room and be recognised as a real creative force on equal terms. I wouldn't have done that with another person who was on their first assisting job. If you don't make space for an assistant to work with your actors early on, and make it clear that this person is making the work with you, then the actors don't necessarily accord that person with enough respect. When working with new assistants, I often make something and then ask them to note what I've done, which is scary for them. But we need to develop a relationship around constructive critique, which includes me being entirely open to their opinions and ideas. I'm just interested in making the best work, and I'll take an idea from anywhere. I'm not a director that comes into a room and goes, 'I know exactly what we're doing.' There is always uncertainty and discussion. I think it's all about discovery. And I have had assistants who have found that very difficult. They've been like, 'But Sarah, you keep changing your mind. You really don't know what you're doing, do you?' Well, no, I don't! I mean, I do. But I don't. And some directors are very disconcerted by that. And when I later see their work, I see that their practice is very different to mine. Which is totally fine – they're just different animals.

As far as you're aware, did the assistants you worked with at the Royal Exchange go on to become successful directors in their own rights?

We used to host a programme at the Exchange called Observer Mondays where people could come into the room and watch, and I have no idea what some of the people who came to that are doing now. But a large number are now making interesting work. Some progressed through the Regional Theatre Young Directors Scheme. Of the people I personally had as assistants and associates, one of them – Bryony Shanahan – went on to run the Royal Exchange with someone else; one of them is running Theatre by the Lake; one of them is running DaDaFest; and one of them is an international associate at the Royal Court. I don't know whether we were profoundly lucky, or whether the experience of being in our room directly contributed to that outcome. I found it equally fascinating when people came to assist or observe and then decided directing wasn't for them. Like one person, for example, went on to become a novelist. I think that's really cool, to be able to say, 'I've tried this and it isn't for me.'

What I find fascinating is that I only actually had one experience being an assistant myself, and it was really bad. It was back in the days when all roads to making work led through the National Theatre Studio. I had made a show to tour schools and someone from the Studio saw it and asked me if I wanted to spend some time as an assistant director there. I didn't understand that the NT Studio was such a big deal, and I didn't have a sense of who the different people were – or anything, really. All I could sense was that my role seemed to involve just sitting there silently and then going for lunch with the director and telling him it was all going really well. That seemed to be my expected input. But I made the mistake of joining in one of the endless, endless discussions around the table, and afterwards I was given a real talking-to about how it wasn't appropriate for me to offer opinions, especially because there were some quite grand actors involved with the show. And I realised there and then that I wasn't the kind of person who could just sit there. I find that very frustrating. And I don't think it's right that anyone should be expected to spend the entire day in a room and not be included – that doesn't sit right with me. But at the time, I was devastated. Then I spoke to someone at the Studio about it and they said, 'Oh, don't worry, it's just that you're not an assistant director.' Which was very useful to know, even though, at the time, I felt I had really failed at something.

Despite not doing the whole assistant thing, you went on to be an artistic director, a literary manager, a teacher, and a very successful director. All of those roles, in different ways, have a sort of nurturing quality to them. Does that assessment ring true to you?

I've always been interested in working with other people. The thing I enjoyed most about being an artistic director was supporting other people to make work. There is no greater privilege than watching, and being close to, someone discovering that they're an artist and finding their own voice. Is that nurturing? I'm not sure. I think I'm just curious about how people make work, and they need to be looked after while they do that. In the past, there has been a lot of guff around what kind of education people thought you needed to be allowed in the room and making work. There was a period of my career when I was really angry about that, because it felt very difficult to make work if you didn't come from that particular background and education. And if you were interested in making work that was challenging or exploring, in my case, the female experience or queer experience, in bigger institutions you could just forget it. So as an artistic director, I felt that I wanted to find a better way of doing things. I don't really like the world 'nurturing', I don't know why. Maybe that says something about me?

No, I couldn't decide if it was the right word either. 'Nurturing' carries with it quite a lot of motherhood baggage, I think…

I think 'enabling' is a better word. I felt quite strongly that sometimes people just needed to be kind of held in what they were doing and told they could do it. I gave them permission, I think.

You mention that moment when someone discovers they're an artist and finding their voice. Did that happen to you? Was there a moment when you really knew yourself as an artist and a director?

Oh, that's a good question! During the early part of my career, I kind of gave up. I directed a little bit, but I couldn't make a living from it and didn't seem to be getting anywhere. So, I became a literary manager, and that's how I first ended up at the Exchange. And it was made very clear to me that I wouldn't be directing there because there was this other exciting young female director there – who, of course, was Marianne Elliott. Bizarrely, it was actually good to not direct for quite a while. Then, when they finally did start to offer me plays, I still thought for a very long time that the truth was I was never that good. People could say really lovely things, but there was a deep sort of imposter syndrome in me. I found it extremely hard to look at my work.

The moment when I finally thought, 'This is it, I've done something there' was relatively far down the line. I made a production of *A View from the Bridge*. It's a great play and we had the right actors at the right moment. But it was the moment when I realised I needed to stop just looking at what was happening on stage and instead look at what it was doing to the people watching it. The Exchange had a relationship with a local homeless centre, and we used to run drop-in drama sessions with them. A guy came to watch the show and sat behind me. It was the second preview and it felt like something was happening. Afterwards, he came up and said, 'Can I ask you a question? How did he know what it was like to be me?' I replied that I didn't know what he meant. And he said, 'How did Eddie know exactly what it's like to be inside my head?' I started talking about Arthur Miller and he was like, 'No. Nobody has ever shown me what it's like to be me.' He was kind of overwhelmed and I thought, 'That is the best thing that could ever come out of a show for me.'

The other formative moment happened very early on after I directed a play in a drama school. It was by Robert Holman – I think he's an extraordinary playwright – and I invited him to come see it, which he did. He talked to the actors and took us all to the pub afterwards. He said to me, 'I think you're very good with actors because you've made them listen. And I think that's the biggest thing a director needs to do: to create a life on stage where people listen to each other.' After that, he was a brilliant mentor to me. I learnt a lot from him about how plays worked and about representing human behaviour and experience. He was also a totally uncompromising artist. He could only make his work in one way: he could never write faster than he writes, and he couldn't do rewrites at all. It's almost holy what happened to him, and I think I learnt a lot about being true to yourself, and how you can only be the artist that you can be. This is an industry where, when you're younger, you're told you need to network and be at press nights and all that stuff, and there's a lot of that looking-over-the-shoulder syndrome. But it was so good for me to meet a man in an anorak who smoked a lot and said, 'You can only be yourself so don't beat yourself up' – and 'Listening is so important.' I was very privileged to meet him when I did.

What led you to theatre in the first place and, thereafter, what kept you coming back?

I didn't do Drama at school, but I was part of a youth theatre in Sheffield that put its plays on in the Crucible. So, my first experience of seeing a play was also being in a play in the studio there. One day we were invited to see the play in the main house, a Howard Barker play called *A Passion in Six Days*, which was about Labour Party politics. I didn't really understand it, but it riled its audience and was quite provocative. There was a moment when quite an elderly actor walked on stage with no clothes on, and it genuinely offended people. I wasn't expecting that to happen, but I found it very exciting – not the naked part, but the fact it made the theatre feel like a dangerous place. Then, when I later came to London, one of the first things I did was see *Road* by Jim Cartwright. That was an absolutely monumental experience, A: Because it was something I recognised; B: Because it was amazing writing; and C: Because it was staged as a kind of promenade performance. I was only eighteen and it was an absolutely full-on experience. I was sat on this chair and right next to me sat an actress who was eating a bag of chips, and then, halfway through the scene, she was sick – onto the chips. And that fucking blew my mind. Just the whole thing was this visceral, emotional experience. It made me go back to the theatre, but it also made me really interested in what actors could do. Even if I don't especially enjoy a production, I am always really interested in watching actors.

And I kept – and keep – going back, because it's like going to church. I'm not religious, but I imagine that, if you are, there are times when you go to church and you're having a crisis of faith, but you keep going to church regardless. In times when I've fallen out of love with theatre, I've kept going because it's just something that I do. And you never know when it will be absolutely astonishing. It's a curious old thing.

Acknowledgements

First and foremost, thank you to all the theatre directors interviewed for this book. It was a sincere privilege, pleasure and source of inspiration to talk to you all. I am especially grateful to Natalie Abrahami who graciously agreed to be the subject of the very first interview which became the 'test' chapter as part of the original pitch. I am also very grateful to the women who generously gave me their time for this book having previously been interviewed by me for other articles. This includes Ola Ince, who has now endured being interviewed by me three times and is always joyful and insightful company, plus Rachel O'Riordan, Natalie Ibu, Tinuke Craig, Tamara Harvey and Debbie Hannan. A special thank you also to Yaël Farber for her patience and wisdom shared over an extended interview lasting three sessions.

Thank you to all at Nick Hern Books, especially Matt Applewhite for your enthusiasm for the project and dedicated hard work to make it a reality.

Thank you to Maddy Costa, as always, for supporting me at each and every new stage (work and life).

And above all, thank you to my husband Lucian for: everything. And to our smiling son, Leo (born: Sep 2022), for being the best reason in the world not to complete a book to deadline.

www.nickhernbooks.co.uk

facebook.com/nickhernbooks

twitter.com/nickhernbooks